MLM Revisited

Fall Back in Love with Your Network Marketing Business

ANDREW R MILLER

Every human being has the freedom to change at
any instant

Viktor Frankl

TESTIMONIALS FOR THIS BOOK

I'm quite open to exploring ways of improving myself and my business and I've read a lot of Network Marketing books, so there was part of me that was wondering if this would just be something I'd heard all before.

I hadn't.

Overwhelmingly, I identified with every single part of it in some way shape or form. It's the only book that I've ever read about MLM where I've identified so much, with such a great proportion of it.

It wasn't instructional. It wasn't telling me how to run an MLM business. Instead it was giving me permission to run it my own way, which is what I have been doing. I'm fortunate, because I have an upline that's given me permission and I'm confident enough to do it, but people who read this book may not be so lucky.

This book gives them that permission to run it their own way. Which is why everybody gets into it in the first place. To be in control. And it's the only book, that I've read, that's addressed that.

It's one of a kind in that it doesn't address the normal "How You Can Be Successful." Instead, it addresses the underlying issues and what everybody feels about it.

Truthfully, only a minority of people are able to work an MLM business the stereotypical way. They're so in the minority, and that's why so many people fall away. Hence, people get disillusioned and you get this big circle of people complaining, giving it bad press and saying it doesn't work and it's all about pressure.

"MLM Revisited" basically addresses that issue and says "Look, it doesn't have to be like that". Yes, there are methods that work but, if it's not for you, it isn't going to work. Therefore, it's not your method.

None of it is rocket science but, prior to this book, there hasn't been anything that has addressed those issues. That's what I loved about it.

In addition, it's short, which is nice. It took me hardly any time to read. It's quite light hearted, but it made some really, really valid points - and it was sectioned really well. I didn't find myself getting lost in any of the chapters.

It was direct and straightforward. No waffle just get it done and move onto the next one.

And the beginning, I think, is brilliant. You know right from the first page whether you should be reading it or not and I suggest that 90% of people who are disillusioned with their MLM business will want to read it.

It's about time somebody gave people permission to not be sucked along with this system that isn't suitable for everybody. You're allowed to do it your own way - and it's the only way you're going to be any good at it .

It might take you ten times as long but, it might not. At least you're actually going in the right direction every day.

I loved it and I would recommend it to everybody. Really good.

Anna Richards - Forever Living

I'm a reflexologist, have been a lawyer for 30 years and I'm also a network marketer with Forever Living.

My major concern around the book was, "Is it going to be another sales pitch?"

I've read quite a lot of MLM books in my time because, obviously, you get recommended to read "self improvement" books.

I found that this book was just so easy to read. It went to the point straight away but in a nice relaxed style. I was really pleasantly surprised about how conversational it is. It was like listening to a person who's just sat talking to me.

You can literally have a cup of coffee, read a few pages, go back to it weeks later and pick up where you left off.

It resonated with everything that I'd experienced in MLM, which is a roller coaster journey, albeit I have total faith in the products, because they've proven themselves to me.

I found the book was a sort of a 'go to' book. Easy, short paragraphs, short chapters which you can literally read for a couple of minutes. It has nice, snappy little sections which all say something that resonate.

As a result, it helped me refocus on my faith in the company

I had been thinking "Is there any point in carrying on? and by reading the book it's made me realise "Actually, yes. Do carry on." It doesn't matter what your individual success is about, just take it as your own journey and stop comparing yourself to other people.

It was quite a personal relationship reading the book. It made me re-examine why I was doing it and I thought "Do it for what you gain out of it, not necessarily what other people gain out of it".

I would definitely recommend it to anybody that's involved in MLM. It has an analytical, easy to understand, style and each person will take something away from it that relates to their particular story or situation.

Jayne Brown - Forever Living

Having been involved in network marketing for the last 20 odd years, I did wonder if this book would cover everything that there is around network marketing and, now that I've read it, I think it's a very comprehensive covering of the subject.

It covers such a miscellany of areas. Nothing in huge depth, because the chapters are all quite short but, there are so many chapters that cover so many different areas, it gives that breadth of coverage. That's what I really like about it.

It's one of these things that, if you've got an issue, then there's a paragraph or a small chapter about that particular subject in there. It'll act as a great reference guide.

I really love the conversational style it's written in. It's like having a chat with somebody over a cup of coffee and you can take a sip of it now and again. It's such an easy read and I think it's very, very informative.

The benefits you get from it depend on the level of experience that people have got of MLM. It would be really helpful for a relative novice; for somebody that's going through some difficulties with their other half; and I've even learned some bits from it and I've been involved in network marketing since the mid-1990s across different companies.

Certainly, from my point of view, I love the training side of MLM and love the camaraderie - it's all about working together. And you get that from this book.

In summary, I found it really helpful, it covers such a breadth of areas and I'd recommend it to everybody.

Kevin Jeeps - ACN

TESTIMONIALS FOR THE AUTHOR

My main concern about working with Andrew was around spending money whilst not knowing whether or not he would be able to help me develop me and my business.

However, as a result of working together, I have become more focussed and more driven. I really liked being accountable to someone else. When you work for yourself it's easy to avoid the things you should do but don't like doing.

It was great working with someone who can draw ideas and solutions out of you by asking the right questions. Andrew also helped me to put a better structure into the business and gave me an unbiased opinion and advice on my ideas before I acted upon them.

I would certainly recommend that others work with Andrew because I believe all business owners and senior managers need a coach to keep us on track and help us develop ourselves and our business. The great thing about working for yourself is that you can do what you want, when you want. The downside of working for yourself is that you end up doing what you want when you want.

Coaching is not a cost. It's an investment in the future success of your business.

Darren Crookes - Herbalife

I met Andrew at networking and immediately liked him. As I got to know Andrew more, I had a feeling he'd be able to help me. To be honest I didn't quite know what to expect, and wasn't sure if it was a good investment financially, but I trusted him so I went ahead.

The first few sessions were very emotional. In a caring, kind and incredibly skilful way, Andrew was able to draw out from me a lot of the 'stuff/baggage' that had been holding me back. I have to admit, I had a bit more stirring me up inside than I'd fully realised.

Andrew is calm, considerate and patient. He just had a knack of knowing the right words to open the floodgates which allowed me to understand better some of the deeper drivers that were affecting my behaviour and ultimately my progress.

Going through this process with Andrew over a number of months has had a huge impact on me personally. I feel like I'm no longer blindly bashing my head against a wall, wondering why I'm stuck and not understanding why I can't move to the next level. There's a clear way forward and I've been able to start enjoying balance and fun in my life again and as a result, of course, my business is picking up too.

Now I've addressed some of the emotional and personal issues, Andrew's guiding me with more practical, strategic business experience and knowledge. This is proving invaluable.

I'd highly recommend speaking to Andrew. You can rely on total confidentiality, a wise and friendly ear, but the right level of challenge to help you move forward in the best way for you.

Elena Delaney - Forever Living

OTHER BOOKS BY ANDREW R MILLER

MORE THAN JUST MONEY
An Introduction To The Business Enjoyment Model *(due 2020)*

MULTIPLY YOUR SUCCESS
The Business Owner's Workbook For Wealth And Opportunity

THE SUCCESSFUL BUSINESS OWNER'S GUIDE TO REDUCING STRESS
How to Avoid These 13 Common Pitfalls

SUCCESSFUL START-UPS
Get Going. Stay Going

HOPE WON'T PAY THE WAGES
How to deal with the personal impact of a struggling business.

All available on Amazon

or at

www.bit.ly/enjoybooks

where you will find more information on each book, along with access to the audio and video versions of The Successful Business Owner's Guide to Reducing Stress.

CONTENTS

ACKNOWLEDGEMENTS

Andrew would like to thank the following people, without whom this book would not have happened.

Elena, Darren, Jemma, Ian, Heather, Salwa, April, Sarah, Janine and, of course, Mary.

INTRODUCTION

Before we go any further, if you're reading this book because you want to earn more money or build a bigger, more successful team, then close it down and go and read something else instead. This is not for you.

That isn't to say that those outcomes might not come to fruition as a result of reading the book – quite often they do – but the focus here is on YOU, not the actual business. I believe that we can all be successful at what we do WHILST enjoying ourselves in the process. That success comes from happiness, not the other way around.

If your focus is primarily on the financial rewards of running a network marketing business, then we're not going to see eye to eye. If your focus is on you and the people you can help, with the financial rewards being a very nice by-product, then we're all heading in the right direction and you should read on.

Since 2011, I have been involved in my own network marketing business as well as working with numerous people in a range of different network marketing systems. Over that time I came to realise that, whilst the network marketing concept is excellent, the process itself naturally creates a huge amount of stress for anyone not perfectly aligned with the system.

The problem with a standard systemised process to

follow is that it doesn't take into account where you are personally. Regardless of which level you are in the organisation, when you get out of kilter with the system, it suddenly becomes hard work. Meanwhile, the promotion machine continues to rumble on:

"Go to the next conference."
"Qualify for the cruise."
"Benefit from the 'top performer share giveaway'."

Although these things are intended to motivate everyone into working harder and doing better, for many people the result is the exact opposite. The motivation creates pressure and the pressure creates stress. That stress then builds and builds until, **suddenly, you realise you can't cope with running the business you love.**

From my own experiences, through conversations with others and by directly helping others get out of this emotional trap, I've realised that the only way to be happy in a network marketing business is to **find YOUR WAY of doing it.**

I've **discovered 28 things** that can be done to improve your relationship with your business and **I know they work** because I've helped others to implement them successfully into their own business.

As a result, they now have the life that they truly want. Happy, relaxed and rewarding.

WHO IS THE AUTHOR?

My name is Andrew Miller and I am the Founder of Business Enjoyment. My purpose is to bring joy back into business and create a movement where everyone is talking about enjoyment as the key measure of success rather than just sales and profits.

I believe that life and business are there to be enjoyed. However, the habits and norms of society have created traps that we all hold within our own minds. They serve as chains that restrain us to a life full of struggle and without fulfilment.

My mission is to break those chains, unlock the traps and lead people to freedom and a life of enjoyment.

I spent over 16 years working for a global accountancy firm in the arena of insolvency. That meant that my main job was to run businesses, but it was done standing next to business owners who were watching everything they had built collapse in front of their eyes. It was a very stark reminder of the emotional connection that exists between a business and its owner.

As for myself, having paid service to the standard route of education and career, I found myself successful and respected, but in a job that I didn't want to be in and came to hate. I realised that, throughout my life, I'd always followed the path that society had expected me to follow; had done things that other people wanted me to do; and generally shaped my world in a way such that I came last in the order of priorities. Doing what other people expected me to do had not brought me happiness, so I decided to go my own way.

In 2012, I published my first book, *Hope Won't Pay the Wages*, designed to help business owners deal with the emotional stress of a failing business. Based on interviews with those that had been through an insolvency, one key factor threaded through them all. Having gone through the worst that business can throw at someone, they all ended up with a completely different perspective on what the meaning of success was.

It wasn't about the money, the cars, the big house. It was about something much deeper. It was there to be enjoyed.

I am building a community of people who want to build successful businesses but enjoy life at the same time. If you would like to know more about the community and how to get involved, then turn to the back of the book and find out about the 'Breathing Space' events that I run.

If you feel incapable of enjoying the success you've had to date; that you don't deserve the good luck you've had; or feel that you just don't belong, then turn to Page 141 or check out my website at

www.businessenjoyment.com

A NOTE BEFORE YOU START

This book often refers to the 'products' that are provided via the MLM organisation. This is a catch all term and also applies to 'services'. They are still a form of product at the end of the day.

Not every point in this book will apply to every person. Some points may be most successful when only partially applied. There may even be some points that appear to contradict each other.

Do not, therefore, treat this book as an instruction manual where every suggestion is a direction that must be followed to the letter.

At any moment in time, each person is in a different place and will benefit from different solutions. The purpose of this book is to help you look at things differently and allow you to try out new approaches.

At the end of the day, you should find a balance specific to you.

It should also be noted that not all of the answers are here. I have no doubt that more out there exist and, over time, I may add to the list. These are just the ones I've go so far.

Some of the things I say may scare you or make you angry.

This is deliberate, as sometimes it's necessary to hit someone hard in order to make a change. If you do come across something that gives you an extreme reaction, this means we've found something really important that could have a major impact on your life.

Step away for a bit, calm down and reflect on what it is inside of you that made you react that way. Then come back to the self same point and face it head on.

Other than that, find the points that resonate with you, that give you a little sense of excitement – that challenge you. Try them out, test them. Feel free to adapt them and make them fit your own way of working. Then keep the ones that feel right for you.

You want to find your way of making things work.

But whatever you do, whatever you try – make sure you enjoy it.

PART 1

Why Should I Bother Carrying On With The Business?

CHAPTER 1
WHY DON'T I JUST QUIT?

This question can arise no matter where you are in your journey.

Whether you're 12 months or 12 years into your business, there is always scope for uncertainty to creep in, confidence to drop and desperation to arise.

Underlying every fear and doubt is the ultimate decision any network marketer can sometimes consider.

Why don't I just quit?

Let's be clear about something from the start. I am not here to be a motivational cheerleader. If things are going wrong and you're looking for me to give you comforting words, pat you on the back and say "There there - it'll be alright" in order to encourage you to get back on the horse - then I'm afraid you're going to be disappointed.

The wrong person in the wrong place is on the fast track to misery and I have no qualms in people jacking it all in, back tracking on everything that they've said and done in the last few years and forging a completely new path – as long at that new path makes them happier.

That's what I did. So has my wife. Many of my clients have. Sometimes with no knowledge as to what the next step will be.

The key question is, of course, how do you tell if you are currently experiencing a temporary wobble or are at the start of a fundamental breakdown of the business relationship?

I suggest your answer is derived by going back to basics.

Do you believe in the product?

For an enjoyable and successful business, belief in the product works on two levels. The first one is pretty obvious. How can you sell anything that you don't believe in? If you want to have a business that you enjoy and can stay passionate about, then it starts with the product itself.

Don't get me wrong, there are plenty of people in the business – very successful people – who are able to get sale after sale after sale – and don't give two figs about what it is they're selling.

Alternatively, I'm sure you know people who research each and every MLM organisation looking for the best compensation package. They start off with one and then jump ship when something that looks better comes along.

For people like that, I say well done. I have no issue at all with what they do and I wish them all the success in the world.

Personally, it's not my way of doing something. It doesn't exactly promote an image of brand loyalty and if I'm going to buy from you, I'm going to want to see just that.

By the way, those people who can sell anything to anyone are a special breed and, to be honest, won't be reading this book.

To everyone else – which means 'you' – belief in the product is everything.

And this is where the second angle comes into play.

If you've been in your business for a while and the system is getting you down. If you've lost faith in the stars on stage at the Annual Conference. If all you hear from your upline is "Why haven't you done this, why haven't you done that?" - then just take a moment and ask yourself this question.

If you weren't doing the business, would you still recommend the products?

If your answer to that is 'no', then you should have a really serious think about whether or not you're in the right place.

On the other hand, if you get a 'yes' from that question, then you have a core reason as to why you do what you do. You have a reason not to quit.

Whenever you face a massive challenge. Whatever your doubts. Whatever your concerns.You can always come back to this critical, fundamental point.

You promote the product because you believe in it.

I know that, by itself, this doesn't remove the challenges. You may not feel comfortable recommending something when you benefit from it as well. You might have concerns about people not being able to afford it. You may see rejection of the product as rejection of you.

There will be hundreds of reasons as to why it will be hard. But at the end of the day, it's all just stuff. And stuff can be dealt with.

Bottom line is, you believe in the product and, of course, care about others enough to want them to get the same benefits that you got.

From this basic platform you can start to build. The rest of this book is intended to help you do that. Yes, you may have to take a few steps back to re-discover yourself. Yes, you might annoy or disappoint some of the people around you in order to get where you want to be.

But if you have a core belief in what you sell, then you can have a business.

All you have to do is to find YOUR WAY of running it.

Actions

Whatever your current situation, I want you to grab a pen and a blank piece of paper right now and do this exercise. Even if it doesn't seem relevant now, it may be invaluable to you in the future.

First of all, imagine that you didn't get any financial benefit from promoting your products.

Now, on your page, write down all the reasons that you can think of as to why you would recommend them to others.

Really take the time to think about what it is that people get from you.

Sure, there are the standard benefits that you have in your script, but really sit and think about your most excited customers. Why are they so ecstatic? Why do they shout about it to others?

Why do **you** use the products? What got you interested in them in the first place? Why do you still use them?

Keep writing answers down, no matter how small they may seem.

When you've got to the point that you can't think of any more ... write down three more.

Done that? Great. Write another three. Just three, go on, you can do it.

Excellent. Then you can find another three.

When you really truly can't think of any more, pause and relax.

Have a think about how you want to manage the list you've just created. You might want to transcribe it into a special book. Or type them up in a Word document and store them on your computer. Maybe just photocopy the original, so you have a back up copy.

I say this as I don't think you're quite done yet. The subconscious brain will be working on the challenge long after this moment and, being the little devil that it is, will be firing the answers out when you least expect it.

When you're out and about prospecting. When you're In the shower. 3am in the morning. You know the kind of thing.

Many of these can be the real gold nuggets, so I want you to keep your list within easy grabbing distance at all times.

Have it in the bedroom for those early morning revelations and the ablution inspired insights. Have it in the car with you or in your bag when you go out and about.

As new ideas come to you, get them down.

Alternatively, use the Note function or Voice Memo options on your phone to record them and then transcribe them when you get home.

Eventually you will have a long list of reasons, every one of which is a reason to carry on doing what it is that you do. After a while, condense that list down to the the top three to five reasons.

Keep the full list for any really dark days that may crop up in the future – just reading through all those positive purposes can change the way you think when you are in a bad place – but put your top reasons somewhere front and centre for you to see.

Now, if you want to keep motivated around your business, use these key reasons in a way that works best for you.

Some people convert the reasons into sentences and develop daily affirmations.

Others write the reasons onto yellow stickies and leave them in obvious places around the house.

I've also known people to create screensavers and welcome messages on their computers and phones.

Whatever helps to keep it forefront of your mind.

The most important thing in any business is to know why you do what you do.

The second most important thing is not to forget it.

CHAPTER 2
WHAT'S THE POINT IF MY OTHER HALF DOESN'T GET IT?

I'm sure we've all been told – and in most cases, discovered - that our friends and family are always the last to buy into the business. But when your other half appears to actively go out of their way to pour water on your excitement and passion, then that hurts a lot more.

Whether it's a snide comment about heading out to 'your thing' again – or questioning whether you've made the right decision and maybe you should consider getting a 'proper job' - living with someone who doesn't share your views can be incredibly draining.

Only, that is, if you let it.

Before I continue, I ought to be clear about something.

I've had a number of clients come to me with complaints about how their other half causes them grief about their network marketing business. Once we've drilled down, we've discovered that the business is just one thing out of a long list and, consequently, not the real issue.

The truth is that their other half is causing them grief, full stop.

As you read this chapter, if you suspect at any time that the issues you have go beyond that of just your business, then stop reading immediately and go straight to the Appendix. This chapter is not going to help you with any fundamental relationship issues that may exist.

However, if you're sure that these disputes are purely centred around your other half not understanding your venture, then carry on.

There are four areas I want to look at:

1) What you're thinking;
2) What they're thinking;
3) What the bigger picture looks like; and
4) How you can actually benefit from the situation.

What you're thinking

The main discussion here is around the concepts of 'expectation' and 'disappointment'.

In a nutshell, 'expectation' is when we think we can predict the future. 'Disappointment' is when we are surprised to discover that we can't.

The antidote to 'expectation', is 'reality'.

Our expectation is that, just because we are excited about the opportunities that this venture can provide for us, then everyone who knows and loves us must also be excited about it.

But when you think about it ... why should they? There's no actual reason why they should.

This is your passion and your vision, and everyone is different. In a relationship, you don't need to share the same dreams in terms of business.

Just because YOU are on board with something, doesn't mean that anyone else HAS to be. Including your other half.

It's ok for them to have different views and hold different opinions – and they don't love you any less for doing so.

If all that you are hearing is negative comments, then that may well be you just hearing the negative element. Their comments will probably be coming from a positive place, even if they aren't very good at communicating them.

Then again, maybe you aren't very good at hearing them.

You see, when we are excited about something and have fully bought into a concept or opportunity, we get blinkered vision about the reality of the situation.

We forget that other people have not gone through the same thought process and journey that we have and, when we are faced with scepticism around something we've emotionally attached to, it is very natural to assume that the attack is directed at us personally.

This leads to us getting very defensive and, before long, an argument ensues.

Instead, take a step backwards for a moment, and consider what they're thinking.

What they're thinking

The natural state of anyone is to resist change. You will probably have resisted the opportunity when it was first presented to you – no matter how long or short that resistance was.

As soon as you try to force anything on anyone, they naturally resist. There's an exercise in Chapter 24 which highlights this perfectly and shows that we are naturally skeptical and instinctively defensive. It is how humans have managed to survive all these years.

In addition, paraphrasing Isaac Newton for a moment, the greater the force, the greater the resistance.

Instead, people prefer to be coaxed. Nurtured. Encouraged. Let them find their own journey.

Treat your other half almost as you would a new prospect. Talk about what's going and find out what their true fears are.

The reality may be that they are scared you'll lose

interest in them. Or run off with someone you meet at an event. It may be something else that you'd never even considered.

What objections do they have and then see what you can do to manage them?

If they get to the point where they understand your excitement, even if they don't see it themselves, then that's great.

I knew one family where the father and daughter were involved, but her husband wasn't. He refused to have anything to do with it and was getting annoyed that all they did was sit around talking about 'the business' and he felt excluded.

Once it was recognised, they tried to help out by restricting discussions around the business to certain times of the day. They even set up a 'swear jar' for when he was there, so that it forced them to talk about other things.

By recognising the issue and taking the fear away, the husband relaxed and actually started promoting the products to his mates. That became his choice, though, not something he was forced into nor something he was expected to do.

So help them with their journey, but don't get attached to what they think or feel about it, otherwise YOUR journey will get affected too.

The Bigger Picture

When we get involved in a one to one disagreement, we often lose sight of what's really going on. What I want you to do is pull back and remember the bigger picture.

Why did you get involved in this business in the first place? I mean the real, underlying reason. How does what you do involve the other person in your life? What is your end goal and does that match theirs?

If your ambition is, for example, to create freedom for you and your family – then that starts NOW – not at some point in the future. The journey is just as important as the destination, if anything, more so.

There is no point in working every hour you can in order to provide a better life for you and your family to then turn round to discover they've left because you were never there.

Are you giving them the attention, time and space that they need right now? That you want right now?

Take a look at how you're filling your days, weeks and months. Have you created space for all the things that are important in your life? Or are they getting pushed out by your desire to make your business work?

Turn that approach around. If your family is that important to you, then treat them, including your other half, as your most important customers. Give them top priority. Make the business fit around them, not the reverse.

If you're getting regular quality time together then you won't feel guilty when you do go out – and they won't feel rejected.

Now you're shifting away from having false expectations of others and starting to make agreements that everyone can buy into.

How you can actually benefit from the situation

Assuming you've discovered and managed the emotional concerns, what you are left with is an excellent potential for exploring new heights.

Talking with somebody who has a different opinion is a great way of improving what you do and how you do it. I call it the Lennon-McCartney effect.

Their contrasting styles meant that they could have blazing rows about how a song was put together, but the aim was always to make the song better, not score personal points. It was this difference in approach that led The Beatles to the heights that they achieved.

And you have that same opportunity sat in your own home.

First of all, remember not to take any comments personally, but know that they come from a position of love and support.

Then listen to what they actually have to say.

Don't reject or accept anything that they say out of hand, but take the information on board and think about it in the context of everything else.

Now you can gain a new perspective on what is going on. Sometimes this can push you in new directions and sometimes it just keeps you grounded.

A relationship is symbiotic. It's give and take, ebb and flow. Even though it may sometimes feel like you're doing most of the giving, this is often just an illusion, as we don't always pick up on everything that the other person is doing for us.

Therefore, instead of trying to change your other half – something which can't be done – appreciate them for who they are.

Celebrate the differences and be grateful for a countering point of view.

That way you truly can be stronger together.

CHAPTER 3
I HAVE TO COMPETE WITH TOO MANY OTHER NETWORK MARKETERS

What we're talking about here is the fear around saturation.

Too many people, selling too many products, to not enough prospects.

Over the various chapters we will actually be addressing this issue from a number of different angles, but here we tackle it head on. It is, of course, all about perception.

Think for a moment about what you're doing to build your business. Possibly going to networking meetings, connecting on social media. And, naturally, going to all the training meetings and conferences that your company puts on.

All of which you've been told to do. The thing is ...so has everybody else. Here is the key thing to remember:

Network marketers go networking.

So you're going to meet them.

At business events. On Linkedin. On Facebook.

At the company training, you're surrounded by

hundreds or even thousands of people who do exactly the same thing.

Then you connect with people that could be potential prospects. How did you meet them? That's right. At business events. On Linkedin. On Facebook.

It is therefore no surprise that they know all about your products and the opportunity network marketing offers, because they've already seen it and tried it.

No wonder the whole thing can feel like a waste of time. There are far too many people out there, doing what you do, for you to be able to make a difference.

The truth is that the desire for the business to be replicable drives similar behaviours which, by its very nature, creates a false perspective on the situation.

When I was younger, I remember listening to a comedy record called "What Goes Up, Might Come Down" by a guy called David Gunson. It was a really funny after-dinner speech around flying and air traffic controllers, delivered in a dry, understated manner. One bit stands out specifically in relation to this situation and it goes like this.

"The reason for having Air Traffic Controllers is a little bit hazy, really.

The chance of two aeroplanes being at the same place at the same height at the same time is so mathematically remote as to be not worth considering.

All you do with Air Traffic Control is to force them down very narrow corridors thereby increasing the risk of collision and thereby justifying the job of a controller to keep them apart "

And that is exactly what is going on here.

You are only getting a very narrow view of what is really going on.

We have to remember that our entire brain is designed to restrict the information that makes it through to our conscious awareness.

Our eyes focus on an area of only around 6 to 7 degrees. Beyond that we have hazy peripheral vision, and that stops at around the 180 degree mark.

Even within that tiny area of perception, there are millions and millions of bits of data streaming around us, all of which are absorbed by the wider brain. Far too many for us to process and deal with.

Consequently our brain focuses and filters, and uses very educated guess work to fill in the gaps and the edges.

So when the we fill our perceptions with row upon row of other network marketers, and only talk to people who have already been in contact with them, then the brain extrapolates that image outwards leading to the automatic assumption that the market is saturated.

Too many people doing what you're doing, trying to sell what you sell to people who already buy it.

The solution of course is, once again, that we ought to look at the bigger picture.

One exercise you can do is to find some statistics about your market place.

Start with your company and see if you can find some figures for how many distributors there are and, if possible, how many active customers. Make sure you know what area those figures are covering. Getting confused between the stats for your 'county' and your 'country' would not be a good thing to do right now.

Now head to the internet and either by Google or Wikipedia, find the population of that same area. As I say, make sure they match. Country for country. State for state.

Then compare one to the other.

You'll find that there will be thousands more people out there that are not part of your business. Even if you include other companies that you see as competitors, the difference is still going to be huge.

If you can truly grasp how big your potential market is, then saturation will not be an issue you have to worry about.

What you do have to think about, of course, is how are you going to meet these people, without going to the standard venues.

The answer here may be to broaden your experiences.

Take up new hobbies. Go and do new things and meet a different set of people.

There are so many different clubs and activities available – many of which are free or very low cost. Walking tours, nature trips, community activities.

All of these contain people that could be your potential market.

However, don't go to these things with a view to selling your product to everyone you meet as quickly as possible. Instead, go with the intention of meeting, and connecting and socialising with new people.

If they ask you what you do, then you can raise the subject and leave it to them to explore deeper, whilst you find out more about them.

Then let them come to you, if they want to.

The reason for this is twofold. The primary objective

is to help change your perspective and see that the market isn't saturated with network marketers.

Become aware of the space that exists around you and make that your norm.

Which means that, when you take part in your standard activities, which you are more than welcome to continue with, you approach it with a new mindset. Now, any other network marketer or prospect who's seen it all before, has a lot less weighting and importance in the world and your reaction will be much more relaxed.

The second reason is, of course, to improve the richness of your life and, in doing so, make the process a lot more enjoyable.

You will probably get clients and team members from these activities, but when you take the pressure off yourself around the obligation to go hunting, then you feel more relaxed and happy. Ironically, you often become more successful as a result.

In summary, stop looking down narrow corridors at all the places that your competitors hang out.

Instead, find new things to do, change your perspective and enjoy the journey.

CHAPTER 4
I'VE SEEN NO EVIDENCE OF THIS 'ABUNDANCE' EVERYONE KEEPS TALKING ABOUT

Abundance. The flip side of the saturation issue covered in the last chapter. Whereas last time we looked at the issue surrounding the business and there being too many distributors and not enough customers, this time we're going to focus more on the abundance concept around money.

We've all read the books and seen the videos. Apparently, it's all about living this life of abundance and letting the energy flow towards us. It's all there for the taking and all we have to do is just tap into it and everything we want will manifest itself into our lives.

Yet, no matter how often we say the mantras or read our affirmations, our brains just won't grasp the concept.

I had one client who felt genuinely bad about her customers paying money to her. Every pound they paid for the product was a pound that they couldn't use on something else.

As a result, she kept discounting the prices, giving things away for free or just avoiding getting new customers.

The concept of abundance can be a hard one to grasp because, whatever contrary belief you may hold around it, you will be able to find an example to back you up.

However, one example, does not create a truth.

Yes, there are people who can't afford what you sell. But that is different to 'no-one' being able to afford what you sell.

Abundance does not mean that, if you try hard enough, then the one specific person you're trying to sell to will suddenly have more money. Instead it means that there will always be a **different** person out there, who **will** have the money.

Money is often likened to being a form of energy. It flows like water does, pooling in some places and running dry in others. But, whilst it may not be actually infinite, as far as you or I are concerned, there is more in existence than we can possibly manage.

Which nicely leads me to a technique that I have found useful to help the brain make the shift and grasp the concept.

Instead of money, think of water.

Whenever you find resistance or concerns around the abundance of money, take some time and write down exactly what your thoughts are and the issues around them.

Then, in those sentences, swap the word 'money' with the word 'water' and read the sentences again.

As a note, you can also use 'air' or 'love', they work in the same way.

If I were to do that with the example I gave earlier on, we would now have the phrase:

"I feel so bad about my client giving me water. If she gives her water to me, then she wouldn't have any water for anything else"

In our society where water is freely available, it totally changes the feeling of the sentence. In fact, it now seems quite ridiculous.

Let's try a few more, common beliefs with our exchange words swapped in. How silly do these phrases seem now?

"Be careful with your love. It doesn't grow on trees"

"Because of what's going on in the world, there's a lot less air about."

"I don't deserve water"

"There is only so much love that anyone should be able to handle"

See how strange those sentences sound?

Many of them don't even make sense once you insert a word that you accept is in plentiful supply.

A simple trick, but it can be quite effective.

Work out what that voice in your head is saying that's stopping you from accepting the abundance that surrounds us and swap in a word that you can accept.

From there you can start getting comfortable with the concept and before you know it, your beliefs around abundance will start to change.

CHAPTER 5
GOALS ARE BAD

There is a famous study that supports the value of goal setting. You may have heard about it. Tony Robbins – you've certainly heard of him – talks about it in his books and seminars.

The 'Class of 1953' Study at Yale University followed the lives of a Yale graduating class over a 20 year period. At the end of that time, it was discovered that the 3 percent of graduates who had set clear, written goals at the beginning, had out-earned the other 97 percent of the class combined.

Impressive, yes?

However. Michael Neill – author of Supercoach and whose work this chapter is based around – was doing some research on a connected project and could find no evidence of this study taking place. Not at Yale, Princeton or any other major American University.

So he asked Tony Robbins, where he got the story from. Tony said "I know exactly where I was when I heard it and who said it. It was Brian Tracy" - of Eat That Frog fame.

So Michael goes to see Brian Tracy and asks him where he got the story from.

Brian said "I know exactly where I was when I heard

it and who said it. It was Zig Ziglar" - another well known American motivational speaker.

Michael then went to Zig Ziglar and asked HIM the same question. And HE said "I know exactly where I was when I heard it and who said it. It was Tony Robbins"

This story appears to be just that. A story. However, we now live in a culture where it's all about goals. You have to set a goal for this. Set a goal for that. Health, wealth and happiness.

"Set a goal – write it down – otherwise nothing will work for you."

And the network marketing industry is about little else.

Now, goals are certainly powerful, yes – but, did you know that they can also do harm? Which is what I want to show you in this chapter. Later on in the book, I'll show you how to do things differently.

Ok. What do we know about goals at the moment?

Most people know one thing about goals. SMART.

Specific – Measurable – Agreed upon – Realistic – Time-bound

Those familiar with this structure, put it around a future based result and then call it a goal. Which is about as far as it goes.

A Real Life Example of a Goal

The example I'm going to use is the England Rugby Union team (no prior knowledge needed).

At the 1999 World Cup, England did not have the best of competitions. They scraped through the group stages and were then knocked out in the very next match. The relatively new coach, Clive Woodward, found his job under threat due to their performance and he had to fight to keep his position. He kept it by making a promise to the public and his bosses, which took the form of a bold, but very clear, goal.

"England to win the next Rugby World Cup in 2003."

Let us check whether or not that fills the requirement of what we understand a goal to be.

It is certainly a future based result, no problem there.

It is certainly very **Specific**.

It can be easily **Measured**. Either they win or they don't.

Take my word for it when I tell you that all the players, the management, the governing bodies and, of course, the fans **Agreed** that it was something they wanted to happen.

It seemed like a huge challenge, but not impossible

if everything fell into place, so it was **Realistic**.

Finally, it had a very clear date in place, so it was certainly **Time-bound**.

A perfect example of a goal.

With this in place, they pulled together a plan to achieve it, built in key milestones and started taking action. Over the course of the next 4 years, the England team worked hard, developed and improved to such an extent that on 22nd November 2003, as had been planned, they won the World Cup !!

So there we are. Goal set. Goal achieved. Everybody happy. What's the problem?

The Problem

The interesting thing is what happened AFTER the goal had been achieved.

In essence, the England team fell apart.

Everything that was created – collapsed. Their annual win percentage instantly dropped from 94% to below 50% and things pretty much stayed that way for the next 12 years. They slipped down the rankings, became a laughing stock and only in recent years have they managed to rebuild and pull together a decent team again.

There are a number of reasons that can explain this

sudden drop in form, but the point is that this 'up and down' effect can been seen all over the place whenever a clear goal has been set.

It happens all the time in sport. Anyone who does something amazing one year, will probably be a no-hoper the year after. Even within a match itself, the most likely time to concede a goal or a point, is just after you've scored.

It applies just as much outside of sport.

If you Google "The Oscar Curse", you can see how many careers have plummeted after they win the big prize.

If you're someone that has to meet sales targets, you may very will hit the level required, but it's virtually guaranteed that performance will drop off immediately afterwards.

Think about how you operate around holidays and Christmas. There's a big effort as you approach and then, exhaustion – and it's hard to get started again.

This is something very common in Network Marketing. How many times have you seen someone work incredibly hard to get to the level they really want to achieve – hit it, and then almost give up once they've got there?

I'm hoping you recognise this pattern now.

Hit goal, fall back. Hit goal, fall back.

This is not the most efficient way to go through life.

The problem is, of course, that as a society, we only look at the point where the goal is reached. It's instilled into us even when we're kids. How does every fairy tale ever written end?

"They all lived happily ever after."

Very rarely is any thought given to what actually occurs afterwards.

Constantly Hitting Goals

Goals DO work – of course they do – but only on a short term basis.

For anything long term, like your business, the standard response is that you just keep setting goals.

Achieve one, set the next. Next sales target. Next objective.

Unfortunately, all you're doing is replicating the same pattern over and over again. Sure it brings results, but each goal requires a huge burst of energy to get across the finish line, which inevitably leads to a crash. Over time, it's draining.

And this, of course, is when you actually achieve the goal.

Missing the Goal

What happens when you don't achieve the goal you set yourself?

Frustrations. Annoyance. You beat yourself up, feel bad and call yourself a failure.

When your bonus structure is all about hitting targets and goals, anything other than complete success is pretty demotivating.

The longer you go on not hitting your goal, the worse it gets and the more you feel like a failure.

Of course, this assumes that you actually want to achieve the goal set.

Hitting the Wrong Goal

Is the thing that you're pursuing actually your goal? Or is it somebody else's?

Throughout life – at school, at work, in life – we frequently find ourselves doing things that other people want us to do. How often do we stop to check that it's genuinely something we want?

I remember an early interview with the tennis player, Andy Murray. As a kid, he was never overly concerned about winning Wimbledon. That was an English tournament and he's Scottish. However, a pressure to win Wimbledon was put on him by the public because it was important to **them**, and suddenly it became important to **him**.

Their goal became his goal. He still achieved it, eventually, but the pressure nearly broke him.

What Are the Rewards?

Then again. Maybe the goal IS your goal. But when you get there, things aren't always what you expect.

Have you ever craved something and worked really hard for it, just to discover that when you actually got it, things weren't quite as good as you'd imagined?

Hopefully, it does actually feel good, but often only for a fleeting moment. The thrill quickly fades.

Remember the last time you got a new car or that smartphone upgrade. As exhilarating as things felt when you first got it, how quickly did the excitement fade until it became just another 'thing'.

Have you ever been on what you think is going to be a dream holiday and then come back saying "Yeah, it was all right"?

When I failed my driving test as a teenager, the pain of failing was much worse than any pleasure I got from actually passing and being able to drive for the rest of my life.

Goals are very often arbitrary benchmarks, artificially generated, or delusions created from fantasy without a full appreciation of reality.

The Standard Pattern of Thinking

Reflecting on the Fairy Tale example of earlier, we live in a world were most people think "If...Then"

If I get this ... then I'll be happy.

If I marry the prince; get the big car; win the lottery; go on holiday; hit that target...then I'll be happy.

When you think about it, that means that you're not happy now.

Usually, if you're not happy now, then you'll probably also find a way of not being happy when you get there.

What is Success ?

With the standard goal model, at which point in the process can you say

"That's it. I've been successful"?

The answer is when, and only when, you hit your goal.

This means that at every point BEFORE you've hit your goal - you've failed.

Every single day.

With goals, you're a failure every day until, eventually, you succeed.

Goals in summary

They demoralise you because you're a failure every day.

The longer that you don't hit the target, the more painful it gets.

If you do hit them, it may not be as good as you thought it was going to be.

It the outcome is what you want, the benefits are usually short lived.

We frequently chase somebody else's goal, which leads to added pressure and frustration.

Finally, every time you achieve your goal, it wipes you out and makes it hard for you to continue.

In short. Goals are bad for you.

There is, of course, an alternative and we will cover that off in Part 2.

PART 2

How You Can Easily Sabotage Your Own Life And What To Do About It

CHAPTER 6
FIND YOUR WAY OF DOING THINGS

As has been mentioned before, a fundamental element of Network Marketing is, of course, that it's a replicable system. Everything you learn, you teach – and so it goes on.

However, 'replicable' does not mean the same thing as 'identical'.

When you try to approach your business in an identical way to that of your upline, you may find parts of it very difficult to do. Continuing to force yourself down that path will just create stress.

The reason is, quite simply, that you're a different person.

Everyone is different and although it has to be 'replicable', you have to find your own style and preferences.

Let me give you an example. Sit yourself down on a bench and spend a bit of time 'people watching'. Specifically, look at how each person walks. We're all doing the same thing – one foot in front of the other. It's a proven system that we've managed to learn and teach from generation to generation. Something that, I would say, is extremely replicable.

Yet, everyone walks differently.

Short steps, long strides, a rolling gait, a mini-trot.

Everyone has found their way of walking which is unique to them. There are, of course, lots of people who aren't able to walk at all, yet they've still found a way to get around.

Everything you do is about finding your own style and adapting your skills and abilities to the situation rather than blindly copying someone else.

If Social Media is not your thing ... don't use Social Media.

If you don't like standing in the High Street interrupting people ... don't do it.

Buying data, email marketing, cold calling, networking. All of these things are recognised and acceptable ways of getting yourself out there – and you get to choose which ones you do.

The best way to build your business is to integrate it into your normal way of life – making a little step away from what you would be doing anyway – rather than a major leap into an arena that really isn't 'you'.

Naturally, I have to bring a bit of balance the other way here.

Anything that you do that is new or outside of your comfort zone, is going to feel uncomfortable at first. That is not a reason to throw it in the bin straight away.

You have to give things a decent go first to distinguish between those things that you can't do, don't want to do or just can't do yet.

The key thing is to make sure you discard the things that aren't 'you', rather than the things that are 'new'.

Do try different things. Explore and test as much as you can and, if you like it, do more. If you don't like it, adjust things and see if you can make it better.

Once you've really played with it and worked with it, then you can make a decision.

Your decision should be based on two things: results and enjoyment.

If what you're doing is getting good results and you're enjoying it, then that's an easy decision to make.

As is the opposite situation where you're not getting any results and you hate doing it.

The other two combinations will depend on where you are in your business right now and what you're prepared to do.

If you're really keen to build some critical mass, you may decide to focus on doing something that garners results at the sacrifice of some enjoyment, just to get some cash in.

Just be aware that this can only be a short term strategy, so make it a conscious decision and give yourself an end date. Otherwise, motivation will fall like a stone.

If you really enjoy a particular approach but the results are pretty poor, well then it becomes a bit of a balancing act.

Will the results come over time? What other approaches are you using? What other methods could you be using if you weren't doing this one? What is your short term objective right now?

As a general rule, the more you enjoy doing something, the more that enjoyment impacts other areas, so this activity could be a 'loss leader' to help fuel energy in other areas.

There is no fixed answer. You're going to have to do some thinking and decision making, I'm afraid. Which is what this book is all about ultimately. You taking responsibility for what you do.

Do things because YOU want to do them. Not because other people are. Not because you've been told that you should. Not because it's the latest fashion.

But because YOU want to do them.

Just make sure you give yourself enough time to make an informed decision.

CHAPTER 7
EITHER GO FULL TIME OR ALIGN YOUR WORK

Broadly speaking, there are three types of network marketers.

There are those who do it full time. This is their primary source of income and every day is spent on building their business, helping their team and pursuing new leads.

Then there are those who do it in their spare time. They have a full time job which pays the bills, and the network marketing is something they do in the evenings and at weekends, frequently with the intention of creating the safety net they need to allow them to leave that job.

Finally, we have the self-employed/multi-business entrepreneur. Someone who has broken out of the corporate world and set up their own business, with network marketing being an additional string to their bow that can help supplement the income.

This chapter is for types two and three: those who have not yet gone full time.

Let me give you two examples of people I know.

Both of them are book-keepers and both of them run a separate network marketing business as an add on. It doesn't matter whether or not the book keeping role is a full time job or their own business, the example applies in both cases.

The first book-keeper's network marketing business is a utility provider. A product designed to save individuals and companies money on their bills, as well as streamlining the service and making it more convenient.

The second book-keeper sells make-up.

Can you see at a glance how one is going to find things a lot easier than the other?

Trying to build a successful network marketing business alongside a different, completely unconnected line of work can be challenging, to say the least.

When there is no link between the two businesses, your focus and your energies are split and you'll end up being pulled from pillar to post, failing to make a success in either of them.

This is especially true when you have other businesses you're in charge of. When you go to a networking meeting or in a social situation, which business do you talk about? Which card do you hand out?

When you talk about everything that you do, it leads to confusion and mixed messages and you leave the listener without a clear handle with which they can remember you.

On a daily basis, which business will you be applying your energy to? Not many people can have the clarity and discipline needed to keep both moving the way they should.

You either have to be very patient or, if possible, find a way of integrating the two.

When there is a natural fit between the day job and the network marketing business, then it is possible to make both flourish.

Think of it like this. Imagine a racing greyhound on a track. It has been trained to chase the hare, and when that bit of fluff-covered machinery comes whizzing by, the greyhound runs as fast it can with one single purpose in mind. Consequently, the greyhound is focussed, fast and efficient.

This time, imagine that the track managed to introduce a second hare running in a completely different direction.

Now the greyhound is confused. It can't chase both. If it focusses on one, the other gets away.

Left to its own devices, the greyhound will either revert to type and focus on one hare, will flit uselessly between each one without making any real progress – or will give up completely.

Chasing more than one thing is hard.

However, if we convert the greyhound into a sheepdog and the hares into sheep, now we have similar animals that naturally flock together. This time, a single dog can keep a group of sheep in check and move them to wherever the dog chooses.

This, therefore, is your choice.

Go full time (focus on one hare) or find a way to get the different businesses to work together (herding sheep).

Sometimes this matching can be quite straight forward.

With our two book-keepers from earlier, because the first one is already talking about numbers and costs they can easily demonstrate how their client can save money. It's an easy shift.

The second book-keeper, however, is going to find it very difficult to shift the conversation from sales and profits to talking about making their lashes look plump and full. They'll still be able to do all of the things that the business teaches them to do – invite people to parties and sell the products – but this is on top of everything else. It is a drain on their resources and energy and they're going to end up exhausted.

Think about the people you come into contact with on a regular basis due to your other job. Whether they are customers, students, parents of students. What are the conversations that you're having with them naturally?

Your objective is to find a question that starts "By the way ..." that will allow you to naturally shift from one business to another.

Anyone in the trades industry can easily talk about utilities. Anyone in the health and fitness industry can easily add healthcare and weight loss products to the conversation.

With other areas, you will have to be a bit more creative.

When I started my network marketing business, the purpose was actually to help support a very specific niche of my coaching business. My target market, by the very nature of the help they needed, had very little money available. Instead of charging them for my time, I was happy to be paid in referrals. I did the same core work and either got paid directly or through the increase in my network marketing business. Either way I got paid and I only had to do one set of marketing.

I aligned the two businesses.

At a basic level, your day job or other business will probably be doing something that makes your clients more money, saves them money or builds personal confidence. Work out which one that is and see how your network marketing business can be interpreted in the same way.

Anyone in the educational arena is building someone's confidence by being more informed. It then becomes a short hop to talk about confidence in how they look – if that is the product you sell.

It might take a bit of work and a few iterations to make the transition feel natural, but once you're able to align the two businesses, the synergies will kick in and you'll suddenly find a whole new reservoir of energy and resources that had previously been diverted elsewhere.

Finally, for those of you who are in a situation similar to the second book-keeper where you have two very different businesses. If you really can't work out how to align them and are feeling exhausted by the additional work required, then I do want you to think very seriously about whether this is this really what you want to be doing.

I appreciate what you want to do and what you're trying to achieve, but burning yourself out is not going to help anyone, least of all yourself.

If you're not going to do your network marketing business full time, then you really ought to find a way to align the two businesses.

CHAPTER 8
SLOW DOWN

The standard network marketing approach to getting customers is all about volume.

Speak to 100 people, then speak to 100 more. Then the next, then the next. Kiss frogs until your lips go numb and keep going, because "Yes" lives in the "Land of No".

You will have team leaders stand on stage boasting about how they went for years without any sleep as they were holding down a day job and then driving all around the country to make a sale. Next prospect, next prospect.

The thing is, whilst this can be a very successful approach when done properly, it is a very old school way of approaching selling. About 100 years ago, when most of the traditional tools were first developed, this was about the only method open to people and became the template for getting customers ever since.

Things have moved on a little bit, but the emphasis is always on 'activity'. The more you do, the more success you'll get.

The problem is, you only hear from the people who made it work. The other 90% - who didn't make it work, who put in just as much effort, who kept their activity levels up, but didn't get the results - their stories are not told.

This does, therefore, tend to skew the message somewhat.

When the focus is purely on activity, without much regard as to what that activity is, then you can fall into the trap of believing that you are being effective by just doing 'stuff'. You end up running around like a mad terrier, generating a load of things, doing a load of work and none of it actually contributing to an end result.

Then, when things aren't working, the natural inclination is to do even more. We are brainwashed to think that the faster we go and the harder we work, the quicker we get the results.

In reality, the opposite is more likely to be true. You're better off by slowing down.

Slow down in terms of activity and slow down in terms of mindset. Recognise that this is a business to be built over time, carefully and considerately. Not a quick win that can be forced for a year or two and then left to work on its own.

You'll recall the tale of the golden goose where the family were happy getting a golden egg on a regular basis. However, in their greed, they decided to kill the goose, open her up and find out how to get all the gold in one go. Naturally, they lost everything by their actions and their actions came from wanting more in a quicker space of time.

They were thinking too fast. If they'd slowed down

and thought more long term, then they would have been extremely successful.

As ever, there is a balance. Sitting around doing nothing won't get you very far. Conversely, if you find something that works time and time again, then you absolutely do more of it.

But if you feel constantly rushed off your feet and have very little reward to show for all of your hard work, then you ought to slow down.

This is particularly relevant if you've got other draws on your time. Family, a job, hobbies.

We are led to believe that the ability to multitask is a desirable and worthwhile skill. The trouble is that it has now been scientifically proved that multitasking basically means 'doing a lot of things badly'.

It is much more effective to focus on a few key actions and make sure you do them well.

The key things to think about when taking a slower approach are:

1) depth over speed;
2) be present; and
3) honour thyself.

Depth over speed

Any successful business comes about by being

scaleable. This means that, as you get a bigger team and more customers, are you still going to be able to service them? If you're running around like a lunatic now, speaking to this person and that person, then it'll only get worse as you grow.

In addition, as you rise through the ranks, the demands on your time become greater as you start getting involved in delivering training and attending more and more events.

Take the time to think how things will work when you do run a bigger team and are more successful. How are you going to keep everyone engaged and maintain the growth of your business?

You should be familiar with the 80/20 rule. If not, go and do some research and come back. In short, if you're doing 100 things right now, then there will be about 20 of those things that will get you pretty much the same result.

What are the twenty things that you should be doing that will give you the best results going forwards? And of those twenty things, which are the four that are the most important? For those that are counting, that's 20% x 20%.

If you did those four things, really well – what could you achieve?

With potential new team members, take the time to get to know them really well. Work out how you can help them, regardless of what you want them to do.

Give them the attention that they deserve.

Build your expectations and timeframes around their desires, not yours. If they say it's going to take a year before they're ready, then let it take a year. By all means, nudge them along but don't force them into something when they're not ready.

Also, are you getting the best out of your existing team? If you spent more time with them and helped them grow their business, would that benefit you more than trying to recruit new members that demand more or your time and effort to get started?

Make sure that you are spending efficient time with them. Make use of technology such as group calls, rather than driving around seeing each person individually. Or record a training video that you can send out to everyone in one go, as well as the next tranche of members that come through.

Does the 80/20 rule apply with your team too? Are there a small number of team members that will deliver much better results than the others, with less input from you. Time spent on these ones will give a much better return on your time than metaphorically bashing your head against a brick wall.

The happiest network marketers that I've met, are those who have managed to build small but strong teams, rather than large, weak ones.

They focussed on depth over speed.

Be Present

It's very important that you stay in the present as much as possible when you're sat in front of your team members and your prospects.

If your head is spinning all over the place, thinking about things that have happened, might happen, might not happen, need to be done and so on, then the conversation becomes about you and your problems, rather than the person in front of you and how you can help them.

When you've got bills to pay and family issues to deal with, it can be extremely difficult to shut out all that noise and switch focus on to somebody else, but it is a practice that you're going to have to keep working on in order to be effective.

When you can get really present for them and focus on what they need, not what you want, then the conversations become much more enriching. Your conversion rates increase and your team members become more engaged. After all, they have their own internal noises going on and they need you to be there to help steer them through. That is not possible when you're distracted.

In all aspects, a key part of life is to always enjoy the 'now', rather than worrying about the future.

I'm not talking about planning here, that is always a good thing to do. I mean that when you are doing something, have all of your attention on whatever that thing is. When the mind wanders to other issues and thinks about things that might happen, you get distracted, and whatever it is you're doing takes longer and isn't as effective.

The past has happened, the future isn't here yet – 'now' is all we have – so learn to spend time in it and enjoy it.

A key part of enjoying the 'now', is recognising what you have and making sure you have time for nurturing what currently exists. Make time for your family, your pets, your team – whatever it is that has helped you get to where you are now. Then, when you do make the time. Be present and enjoy the moment.

If you are struggling to block out the external noises and stay in the present, you may want to consider exploring some mindfulness courses. There are plenty of good value books and courses around. The whole point of mindfulness is to become aware that we are separate from the thoughts that fly around in your head. Once we grasp that, we can start to pick up and put down thoughts and emotions at will and choose to ignore those that don't serve us in this moment.

It takes a while to get to that stage, but every step taken is one in the right direction.

Honour thyself

Standard practice is to allocate all our time to things

that are important to us and then forget the most important thing of all. We forget about ourselves.

The reality is that there is an inner child within all of us that will end up resenting us if we don't give it at least some attention now and again.

Not only is it ok to sit down of an evening, have a glass of wine with your other half and watch the telly – it's actually important that you do so.

When our inner child feels left out, it finds ways to sabotage us. This may be through making us ill, enforcing anxiety attacks or just removing our motivation.

Even if you can only find one hour a week for yourself, take that time to make yourself feel good, whatever that looks like for you, and everything else will benefit as a result.

Summary

Contrary to what you have been taught, quality is much more important than quantity. If pushing hard and fast isn't working for you, then do the opposite and explore what happens.

Short, concentrated bursts of the right things tend to be much more effective than constantly running around and much less likely to lead to burn out.

Slowing down is often the way to move ahead.

CHAPTER 9
AVOID SCHIZOPHRENIA

When you take on a network marketing business, what you don't realise is that you actually take on responsibility for three different elements.

When you are 'selling' your product or the opportunity that can be achieved by the person in front of you and that person says "No", there are three things that they could be saying "No" to:

1) You;
2) The Product;
3) Other Network Marketers

You

This is the category that most people leap towards when they've just been knocked back, even though it is the one that is least likely to be valid.

We find it very easy to take rejection personally and our default setting is often to assume that it's something about us that has turned them off. If we are walking into situations with this belief running around in our heads, then continued rejection is going to result in a massive dent in our self worth, self esteem and self confidence.

I am sure there must be some people out there that create instant repulsion in others but, even if those people do exist, I wager that they don't create that reaction in everyone.

By all means, check that you're showering regularly and not being offensive every time you open your mouth but once those things are ticked off, the reality is that most people can get on with most others for a reasonable length of time.

There are so many reasons why somebody might say "No" and I'll tell you now, it never has anything to do with you.

The Product

We'll look more at this in Chapter 21, but the reality is that some people just aren't interested in the product, and that is ok. Not everyone wants to buy everything.

Once again, of course, we do often throw a bit of ourselves into the mix. If you believe in the product so much, then it means that it is entwined into your beliefs and values.

Hence, a rejection of the product is seen as an attack upon those beliefs and values and, therefore, upon us.

This is, of course, only in our own heads.

The other person has no idea what you're thinking. They just see a bottle of stuff that they don't have any interest in and, therefore, have politely declined your offer. They are not attached to it in the same way you are.

Other Network Marketers

Finally, when you hear a "No", it may have absolutely nothing to do with you, or even your product.

Human beings do love to stereotype, which means that, to some people, one network marketer looks just like any other. They will see no difference between the opportunity you offer and the opportunity being offered by someone else they met, even if the product is completely different.

As well as closing their minds to what's in front of them, if they were unfortunate enough to have had a bad experience with a different company or distributor, then it may be those people that they are rejecting, and you just happen to be in the firing line.

It's not fair and it doesn't help you build bridges with them, but it's a fact of life.

Just ask estate agents.

Summary

Instead of driving yourself mad and assuming that every rejection is targeted at you, take a moment to recognise the different aspects of your business and embrace them.

Recognise how many reasons are out there for people to say "No".

If you can find ways to deal with those objections in advance, then you're going to dramatically increase your chances of getting a conversion.

However, the point I want to impress here is that you should let all of these other reasons take the brunt of any rejection you encounter.

The alternative is not pretty.

CHAPTER 10
DEFEND YOUR CONSTRUCTION

How often do you get distracted from doing what it is that you really want to do? You end up focussing on priorities set by other people and you allow them to take control of your daily schedule. This leads to a lot of work being done for the benefit of others meaning that you, and those you care about, are the ones that suffer.

Time management, procrastination, distraction, avoidance – call it what you will, it's probably one of the biggest issues for anyone, anywhere.

At the heart of the problem, usually, is that we find it very difficult to say "No" to others. We want to help others and, when your help is asked for, it feels wrong and downright rude to say anything other than "Absolutely, when can I start?"

I developed the following imaginary scenario with one of my clients and it really helped them to create their boundaries and keep them. Hopefully, you'll find it useful too.

I want you to imagine that you're in charge of a large construction site and you're building a huge tower which represents the life you want to lead.

This building is, of course, built on foundations and, in this case, your foundations are the things which are most important to you.

You family. Your values. Your own wellbeing.

Just take a moment to think really deeply about the things that are really important to you. The rest of your life is going to be built on them, so it's best if they are clear, strong and dug deep.

The construction process cannot properly start until these foundations are in place. Then, as long as you keep them intact, the tower that is your future can be safely built.

Of course, at this stage, we only have the foundations – the future is yet to come. Consequently, any construction site worth its salt is going to protect those foundations from any vandals and terrorists that might want to damage them. So you put up fences around the edge of the site, install CCTV cameras and have guards with dogs patrolling the perimeter.

Going forward, the strategy is simple.

Only let through the access gate and into the compound, people and things that are going to help you build your tower.

Those that will add to your energy, build on your vision, contribute to your growth and, of course, believe in your values.

On the flip side, anyone or anything that might damage the foundations or slow down the building programme, should be kept out.

These are the people who want you to work on their projects, that want you to spend your time on things that help them and not you. Instead of adding, they drain you of energy. Time wasters, negative people, poor team members.

Do not let these people into your compound !!

If anyone does sneak past the guards, get them out as quickly as possible.

Are you clear about what you're protecting? Do you know why you're protecting it? Do you know where the threats are going to come from?

If those threats persist, are you prepared to set the dogs on them?

Think really deeply about this scenario and, when you find someone asking you to do something that is going to waste your time, bring this memory back up.

Now see how easy it is to say 'No'.

CHAPTER 11
DON'T HIT TARGETS, ENJOY THE ACTIVITY

In Chapter 5, we looked at the down side of setting goals. As a quick recap:

They demoralise you because you're a failure every day.

The longer that you don't hit the big figure, the more painful it gets.

When you do hit them, things often aren't as good as you thought they were going to be.

When they are as good as you thought, the benefits are usually very short lived.

In short. Don't set goals.

I did say that I would talk to you about an alternative approach and there are certain people you can look at that clearly have a different outlook on life.

Instead of the England Rugby Team who struggled to win one tournament and then fell away from view, you could look at the All Blacks that are consistently the best team in the world and continually work on getting better and better.

Instead of the business owner who gives up when things get tough, think about the 'Richard Branson's of the world, that keep starting up new company after new company, knowing that some will fail and some will succeed.

The really successful people keep progressing and progressing. Always improving. Always moving forwards, and seem to be enjoying what they do at the same time.

What do they do that's different?

The Alternative Approach

The traditional concept of goals is all about finding a place to get TO. Somewhere else that you need to be in order to be successful. When you think about it, this takes value away from the present. Those who develop a different approach find a place to come FROM.

The future based "If ... Then" approach we talked about before, doesn't apply to them, as they work on who they need to BE to get what they want, and START there.

Take the heavyweight boxer, Muhammed Ali. Known around the world as "The Greatest".

This title was not bestowed upon him due to the things he achieved.

And he didn't set a GOAL to be the greatest. What

would that even look like?

When he first started out, he couldn't have said "IF I do this, THEN I'll be the greatest". It wouldn't have made sense.

Instead, HE decided that he was the greatest. Not in the future, based on some prescribed formula, but right from the off. He knew it and he told everyone – whether they listened or not.

FROM that place, he did great things. Then everyone listened.

Emotional attachment

There are two elements I want to introduce you to that explain how we react to situations. One is Dependency and the other is Influence.

'Dependency' is how much you rely on something to impact your mood. 'Influence' is the level of control you have over it.

The table below shows the four ways that these two elements can interact with each other.

Low Influence High Dependency	High Influence High Dependency
Low Influence Low Dependency	High Influence Low Dependency

Low Influence. Low Dependency.

Let's imagine someone who hates football, watching a premiership match on television.

They have no influence over the outcome and, at the same time, don't care about it. Regardless of the result, they won't get stressed in any way, neither will they get excited.

People permanently in this box don't have bad lives, but they aren't great either.

Compare that to an avid fan watching their team play. In this case we get:

Low Influence. High Dependency.

As the game ebbs and flows, so do their reactions as they either cheer and whoop, or shout and scream at the television. If their team wins, they're happy for the rest of the day. A bad loss and they are in a grumpy mood for some time.

In other words, their emotional state is completely dependent on the outcome.

Yet their influence is no greater than the first example.

Another example is when you have work piled up so high you just can't see how you can even make a dent in it. 2,000 unread emails in the inbox. Calls coming in left, right and centre. Papers piled above your head.

You really want it to be done, but nothing you do seems to make a difference. It's only a perception, but it feels real.

Living in this box leads to feelings of frustration and helplessness, possibly anger.

High Influence. High Dependency.

This is where the 'driven' people sit. Determined to make things happen regardless of who they hurt on the way.

The power hungry CEO. The archetypal sales person. 'Those' network marketers I mentioned in Chapter 1 – that won't be reading this book.

"Must get to the next level, must make the next sale. Go, go, go. High energy. High effort. High reward."

That is, of course, how it works in the extreme corner of the box, but most people are encouraged to live somewhere in this area. The meritocracy system of exams, interviews and performance bonuses have conditioned us to place ourselves here.

It's from this place that most goals are set and where we get the up/down pattern described previously. Something that is not easily sustainable long term.

Which leaves us with one last box.

High influence. Low dependency.

You have control over what happens, but it isn't going to have an impact on how you feel.

Those living in the previous box would probably say that you don't care about the outcome. That might be true, but only grammatically.

What it means is that you are coming from a place where you do things - not because someone else says you should. Not because you HAVE to. But because you WANT to. You CHOOSE to.

Which also means that, if you choose not to do it. At any point. That's fine too.

People coming from this space don't set a goal. They set a direction.

The ultimate end point of the destination is much higher than any goal they may set. Which is fine because, what is critical is that they know they may never actually achieve it.

Like being "The Greatest", it isn't a binary thing that you are or you aren't. Achieved or not achieved. It means that it doesn't matter how good you are, you can always get better.

When you're not emotionally attached to the

outcome, you are free to be who you ought to be right now. The only thing you think about is heading in the right direction.

This may be a number of little actions or projects – some of them can be tiny – but they all move you in the right direction. All you do now is select the projects and actions that you enjoy doing the most.

Daily success

When you find a direction you choose to go in and projects that you enjoy doing, then look what happens.

Every day you do things that you like doing and every day it moves you in the right direction.

Remember how traditional goals worked?

They were set in the future, so were something you worked towards. It was all about the result, which meant that you were a failure for the majority of the time, and the outcome wasn't all that great anyway.

With the High Influence, Low Dependency approach, the focus is on now. You do things you enjoy every day and can be successful every single day. You're not relying on a future result to bring happiness, so you can choose to be happy now.

There is no build up of pressure, no success hangover – just consistent, enjoyable progress.

I appreciate that it can sound a little simplistic but, ultimately, it's a mindset. As with all mindsets, it's not necessarily that easy to shift, so you may need to keep working on it.

To help grasp the concept here are some examples.

Example 1

Imagine an oak tree.

Its purpose, its direction, is to stay alive as long as possible and produce as many acorns as it can during its lifetime.

Every day it continues to grow and continues to do whatever it needs to do produce acorns, and keeps doing that until it can't do it anymore.

To me, that seems very obvious and straightforward.

If, however, I were to ask you "What is the 'goal' of an oak tree?" what answer could you give? Especially if you try to conceive a SMART goal.

Sure, you could set it a target of 100 acorns this year, and 120 acorns the next but, in reality, the question doesn't even make sense.

Why should it be any different with us?

Example 2

Let's look at the global space programme.

Back in the 1960s, there was the so called Space Race between the USA and the Soviet Union. Whilst the USSR got the first man into orbit, it's generally regarded that America won the Space Race by getting the first man on the moon and, critically, returning him safely to Earth.

These days, anything to do with research or exploration is all centred around the International Space Station. With the exception of a few independent programmes, all space travel, all future plans for expansion – even the discussions around missions to Mars – all rely on this single, remarkable feat of engineering.

As America 'won' the Space Race, you would think that they would be running the show when it came to all things 'space'. However, that is not the case. It's actually the Russians that are in control.

Sure, they co-operate with other countries, but the technology, the creation and the running of the space station are all down to the Russians and it could be argued that they are the real winners – or at least, way out in front at the moment.

This is because the moon landings were a 'goal'. A clear, specific outcome that everyone worked towards. Sure, the Russians were on the same track to start off with and weren't far behind the

Americans when Neil Armstrong hopped onto the lunar surface.

Once again, the interesting bit is what happened afterwards. After the Americans landed on the moon, they kept returning. Essentially repeating the same goal over and over again.

The Russians, however, immediately dropped all plans on going to the moon and, instead, focussed on general space expansion.

The Space Station concept is just a staging post in the overall direction they're heading in, which is to get further and further from Earth in a manageable way. There is no point where they can go "That's it, we're as far away from Earth as we need to be now. We'll stop." Other factors may intervene to divert funds away, which will stop progress, but, until then, it's a permanent ongoing process.

In short, the goal setters hit their goal and lost out on the bigger picture to those who set a direction.

Example 3

Final example is a coaching acquaintance of mine who adopted this directional approach when he wanted to lose weight and get fit.

The traditional method is, of course, set a target weight and a timescale, pull some actions together in terms of going to the gym and cutting down on food. Then resent the effort and feel miserable every day, because you're being deprived of what you want and, eventually, give up.

Alternatively, maintain the discipline, hit the target and, within three months, put it all back on. The classic, yo yo diet that we're all familiar with.

Instead, he used the directional method.

First of all he thought "Who would I have to be in order to be the right weight and fitness?"

The answer is quite obvious of course. Someone who eats healthy and someone who regularly exercises. That then is a place to come from. Be that person now.

The next thing was that he split the overall direction into two separate projects:

Project 1 - lose weight. Project 2 – get fit.

Connected, obviously, but actually different. The key things was to focus on just the one to begin with, to avoid overwhelm.

For that first project, he set himself one action. Just one.

"Every meal, make it healthier than the one before."

That's it. Nothing drastic like cutting out all sugar or fat in one stroke. Just make tiny steps in the right direction. Maybe it's a smaller portion, or swapping in mash for chips. Next time, veg.

It was his choice what he did. Any small step was a success and it didn't need to be onerous. As the changes were only little, his enjoyment of the food wasn't really impacted.

One discipline. One action. Small effort.

After a while, this became a habit, at which point he brought in the second project. He had a bike, although he couldn't really get very far on it. Nevertheless, his second action was

"Whenever I get free time, ride the bike."

Didn't matter if it was only 10 minutes round the block. If there was a gap, get on the bike.

After a while, this became a habit as well and, eventually, he wasn't giving any thought to what he needed to do, it just happened.

In 9 months, he lost 4 stone and was regularly cycling 10 miles a day.

This came from just two simple actions done consistently that took tiny steps in the right direction.

And he enjoyed himself every step of the way.

Summary

Give up on the goals, but don't give up on the actions. Find a direction that feels important to you. It helps if it is something you emotionally connect with.

Think about yourself in the future, having travelled much further in that direction. Who would you have to BE in order to be that person. What can you do to be that person NOW?

Coming from that place, what tiny steps can you take that will move you in the direction you want to go?

Avoid overwhelm by focussing on one or two daily actions that will move you forwards and are either fun and easy, or at worst, not too onerous.

I will leave you with two actions that, if you follow these, will see you right every time.

1) Every day create one meeting with a prospect. That's it. Just one. Just do that every day.

2) Every proposal you make, sell more than the previous one.

Those two actions, done consistently over time, will create wonders. Remember, happiness is not a destination, it's a journey.

PART 3

How The Wider Company Fuels Your Insanity And What To Do About It

CHAPTER 12
STOP COMPARING YOURSELF TO OTHER PEOPLE

"I've been doing this business for 6 months now and all I've got to show for it is a handful of team members who don't do anything and a few clients who only buy the absolute minimum."

"I heard that Diane has a team member that's only been in for 6 weeks and has already done enough to get to the second level. That is ridiculous. I must be doing something really wrong."

Sound familiar?

The biggest mistake any network marketer can do is to start comparing themselves against others.

Easy to say, hard to do. It's human nature after all.

But do try to remember the key thing. You don't have all the facts.

You don't know where they've come from, what they do, who they know. You don't know how much time they spend on it. You certainly don't know how stressed they are, as they'll never admit to that.

Freud coined a phrase "The Narcissism of Small Differences" to describe the following observed behaviour.

Those people closest to each other are the ones that are most likely to ridicule each other and develop feuds (think the British and the French as a simple example). We develop a hypersensitivity to tiny details of differentiation.

When we see someone doing well in a completely different field, such as science or sports, we can appreciate their achievements without feeling jealous. The closer someone comes to our own circumstances, the more likely we are to resent them. Even though the differences between us may be, in reality, vast.

For every senior team member with a flourishing business and a truly fantastic home life, there is another who is hiding a failing marriage, with stress levels way over their head and on the fast track to burnout.

In some cases, you have to ask the question, are they even doing things legally?

I have seen so many 'wunderkids' that have been lauded by their upline and their team members, hailed as the second coming and on the fast track to becoming a millionaire. Then, just as quickly, they disappear in shame and embarrassment as it turns out that what they were doing wasn't 'appropriate'.

Over everything else, you just have the natural ebb and flow that differs with every person. We all move at different rates and in the long run it all averages out.

Here's a thought exercise you can undertake to illustrate the point.

Imagine you're driving on the motorway.

Pootling along at a speed that's comfortable for you. You find yourself overtaking some people at various points and, at the same time, you are regularly being overtaken by other drivers coming up from behind.

Take a moment to think about each driver.

Think about how some of them are going slower than you, whilst others are going faster. Much faster in some cases. What emotions does this bring up for you?

Hang on a mo though. What do you genuinely know about the other driver?

How long have they been driving for?
Where is their final destination?
Why are they on the motorway at all?

First of all, you'll start to realise that you all have different journeys to take and no-one can truly know what anyone else is thinking.

Then, just as that is sinking in, you look up and ...

SMASH !!

... you plough straight into the back of the car in

front.

Focus on **your** journey and not the journey of others

CHAPTER 13
DON'T FOLLOW BLINDLY

There are so many tips and suggestions that go flying around the circuit that it is very easy to get drawn up in the enthusiasm of it all.

I remember a couple of years ago when vision boards had a resurgence in a certain team. Suddenly, everyone was creating their vision board, talking about their vision board, telling their team that they HAD to do a vision board.

Hang on a sec. Will a vision board actually work for you?

Do you know if your learning preference is of a visual nature? How do you adapt the process if you're more of a kinesthetic or an auditory person?

Even if it will work for you, have you got the space to display it effectively? Are you aware you have to keep updating it?

There are so many things out there to try and do – and I'll always encourage the experimental mindset that will explore new things. Definitely use the tools you're given to learn and feel free to copy what others do.

But don't do it blindly. Think before you act.

Are you choosing to select the ideas that you think might work for you or are you just getting on the bandwagon and doing it because everyone else is?

The more you get to know about yourself, the more you'll be able to get a feel for what will work for you. Then you can filter out the less likely ideas and save yourself a lot of time.

If you truly have no idea, then give it a go but be prepared to drop it if it isn't working.

The more selective you can be about your learning paths, the more likely you'll be to find the one that works for you.

CHAPTER 14
BEWARE INSPIRATION

How many times have you been to a National Conference Day and come away buzzing and skipping with all the inspirational stories and the great messages delivered from the top of the stage? You've bought the latest gadget or product that will help your business boom and have a head brimming with new ideas and action points.

Then you get home, go to bed and a few days later you're in exactly the same place, except you've now got a load more work to do and you're surrounded by a load of useless crap that you wish you hadn't bought.

Externally generated inspiration can be short lived and is often used to manipulate us into doing something that we might not have done otherwise.

On the other hand, if you can find internal inspiration - the thing that makes you realise why you do what you do every day - then that has some staying power.

So yes, do go to the events and do feed off the energy. But don't get carried away by it. Be selective about what you pick out as learning points and only use what will genuinely help you.

Then, become selective about which events you go to. Despite being told you NEED to turn up to every single conference, every monthly 'gathering' – you don't. Once you start feeling obliged to be there, it then becomes a chore and you become resentful.

In the same way that Chapter 12 explained that you can't know what's going on for other people, neither can other people know really what's going on with you. They don't understand your priorities.

Plus, the people behind the scenes do put in a lot of work to come up with something new at these events. Which is great. But it also means that you end up getting overloaded with information. New tactics to try when you haven't got round to testing the last lot. This leads to confusion and uncertainty.

You want new ideas to come to you occasionally, not frequently.

When you are given a load of new things, notice what does give you a tingle, give some thought about what inspired you and look for the specific thing that caused it. Look beyond the story itself, break it down and find the messages within that gave you energy.

There will be something that you are doing right now with your life that will be replicating a part of that message. It might only be a small part, but it will be there.

When you focus in that area, then you don't need to go to conferences to be inspired. You'll inspire yourself every day.

CHAPTER 15
REMEMBER THE REAL REASON

Once you get into the network marketing world and are focussed on selling your products and building your team, it's easy to forget the bigger picture.

Everything you do makes more money for the people above you, ending of course with the guys at the top

No issue with that, that's the entire concept right there. Plus, it works for you too, with those in your team helping contribute to your financial wellbeing.

But beware the downward pressure that comes from on high. It starts right at the top, trickles down all the layers and by the time it arrives at you it is just 'the thing that is done' and not questioned. But it feeds their agenda, not yours.

I know you want more money, but there are other things that you want too. Don't be afraid to strive for these as well.

Are you too busy seeking approval from others to focus on yourself?

The system is often set up so that exclusive clubs are created which require you to be at a certain level before you can come in. Is this about you getting what you genuinely want – or just looking good in front of others?

Once you see through the spin and PR you realise that it gets back to the point about internal inspiration. If you measure yourself by what other people do or think of you, then you walk a dangerous line.

Let me be clear. I'm not knocking the integrity of those above you. With a few very minor exceptions, I believe that everyone is genuinely sincere. The issue is when thoughts become dogma instead of true opinion.

All I want you to do is make sure that you do it for you, not the guys at the top.

PART 4

How To Actually Enjoy Prospecting

CHAPTER 16
COME FROM WANT, NOT NEED

You will have a hard time getting anyone on board; client or distributor, if your own mind is occupied with your own needs.

"I **need** this sale. I **need** the money so badly. I can't afford to lose them. I'll drive 40 miles to hand deliver the products just so that they sign up."

If you're in this space, what happens if someone shows the slightest bit of interest? Do you hound them in the follow up?

"Just checking in. Touching base. Do you want to buy my stuff? Do you want to work with me? Please say Yes. Please!"

Take note of your mental state whenever you're interacting with a potential client or team member.

Watch out for thoughts that suggest that this one person could change things for you.

"When this person joins, then I'll make it. I just **need** to keep working on them. I'll pop round to their house and see how they are. I'll talk about them to other people. I won't switch focus onto someone else just yet, I want to make sure that this person gets on board first."

Let me tell you a phrase that I hear so often from people who have recently set out on their own.

"This **has** to work."

Really? "Has" to? Words like "need" and "has to" are very interesting and powerful pieces of language.

Granted you "want" it to work. But "has" to work?

"Yeah, but you don't understand. If this doesn't work, I'll lose my house. I'll have to go on the dole. I'll have to move back in with my parents. People will laugh at me!!!!"

Yes? So what?

Everything listed above is all about pride and ego; about things being a bit uncomfortable for a while. There are no actual lives at risk, or even a physical threat to deal with.

The Power of Context

Let me be clear, I'm not saying any of the above are desirable. They're definitely not going to be put high up on today's "To Do List". However, there are very few things that we genuinely "Have" to do.

It's worth noting that any phrase that features "Need to" or "Have to" always come with a context or a rider based on a choice.

"If I want a certain thing, then I need to take a certain action"

"I need to go to the bank - if I want to pay this

cheque in."

"I need to go to the shops - if I want to buy some food today."

Within that context the word "need" makes sense. Drop the second half and suddenly it causes confusion.

"I need to go to the bank!"
"I need to go to the shops!"

These phrases now sound much more urgent and desperate. The element of choice has disappeared and it has shifted from a preference to a demand.

When you use these phrases in isolation, go back and add in the second half and see what happens. Having the full context can shift things quite a bit.

"I have to keep breathing, if I want to stay alive."
"I have to eat, if I want to stay alive."
"I have to carry on living in this specific house if I...want to...erm, be in this house" – hang on that doesn't quite work.

Now that we have the context we can look at the situation as reality rather than an abstract concept.

Worst Case Scenarios

There is genuine power in exploring worst case scenarios and playing them through as far as you can. Much of the panic is caused by not knowing what might happen and subsequent over-dramatisation. Reality can be tough, but not actually as bad as we might think.

What would genuinely happen if you lost your house? Again, I'm not saying this is a strategy to target. I'm asking, if the absolute worst happened, and you lost your house, what would actually happen?

The truth is that you'd be heavily inconvenienced for a while and then you'd sort something out.

I remember listening to a podcast where a multi-millionaire was being interviewed. Part of his story was that his first venture made him a fortune, but then got hit by the crash and he lost everything. He had to sell up and at the age of 32 ended up living back with his parents. Sure he didn't want to do it and it wasn't great by any stretch, but the reality was that he dealt with it, got over himself and started again.

Change your mindset

What happens when you are in a place where you think something "has" to work is that you put pressure on yourself. You become desperate. You become needy.

And it doesn't work.

If you have this sense of extreme need in your mind, then your language and your behaviour is going to push others away. You don't want to be needy. You want to be the opposite of needy.

You want to know that you'll be happy to work with them, that you actually WANT to work with them, but only if they're properly on board.

Ideally, you want **them** to be needy.

Take your time exploring their world. Work out what their drivers are and what's important to them. Find out how you can help them – even if that means NOT SELLING THEM ANYTHING.

You can only do this if you're coming from a place where you want to help them, but are relaxed either way.

They will decide in their own heads if they like and trust you. Like and trust the product. Like and trust the system. Let them make the sale themselves.

Get them interested, give them the information and let them come to you.

If you push someone to join before they're ready, you end up with a difficult team member that never performs, or a customer who falls away. These end up taking your time and energy, so better to filter them out early.

A small, well performing team, looking after a handful of loyal customers, is much more powerful than a huge team that never gets out of the starting blocks.

Which means you can't build the team or the business you want if you're in a mindset of "this has to work".

Naturally, the best thing to do is be in the position where everything is NOT riding on it. That may mean you choose to do something else to keep the income up whilst you get the business off the ground. Get a part-time job, stack some shelves. Whatever it takes so that the pressure is removed from you and you can sit in front of somebody that you want to and put their needs first.

Whether it's changing the situation or changing your mindset, make sure you do things because you WANT to do them, not NEED to.

CHAPTER 17
BE GENUINE

It is very easy to fall into the machine that is the system and forget who you are and why you actually got involved in the business in the first place.

You're given scripts to learn, selling techniques, verbal cues to look for and very soon everyone is saying the same thing, the same way. Like a robot.

Stop all of that, now!

This is a human being in front of you, not a computer that will blindly follow whatever instructions you give it. The more you sound like a standard sales pitch, the less likely you are to engage. The more uncomfortable you'll be in delivering it, the less successful you'll be.

Instead, be genuine. Be yourself.

Relate to them as a person by being a person – with all the flaws and problems that go with it. Your inherent belief in the product, will shine through without a prepared speech.

Not that scripts are banned. They are a good way of thinking about what you want to say in advance, just make sure the words come from you and not someone else.

Then, just be honest about them. If you do want to get some certain key points across then say so.

"There is a requirement for me to mention some key things and there's no way I can remember them. Mind like a sieve, me. So I've got them written down. Is it OK if I just read them out and then we can get back to the conversation?"

Make it clear that a 'No' is ok. You're only giving information and you can stop at any time.

I've had some distributors get a piece of card, Red with 'No' on one side and Green with 'Yes' on the other. Show them the card and put it Green side up but tell them that if they want you to stop and go at any stage, all they have to do is turn the card over.

If you make it easy for them to say 'No' it takes the pressure off and either saves time because you get to 'No' quicker or, ironically, increases the chances of them saying 'Yes'.

Think how you like being sold to – or not! What would you want to hear from the mouth of a salesperson that would make you more inclined to buy? What makes it easier for you to reach a decision comfortably?

What works for you will work for others, so don't be persuaded to use someone else's words and actions.

You're looking to build a relationship, not make a quick sale, so respect that relationship and be honest, open and genuine.

CHAPTER 18
FIND A TARGET MARKET

When it comes to selling anything, there are two types of people in the world.

There are those who seem to actually enjoy rejection. With skins as thick as a rhino's, they 'Go for No'. More than happy to receive a metaphorical slap in the face, time and time again, they just keep bouncing back, asking for more. Insults, character assassinations, death threats – nothing will stop them from approaching a stranger or chasing a lead.

Then, there's everybody else.

I'm going to take a punt here. I reckon you're in the second category.

Interestingly, when you first joined the company, you were told to approach anyone and everyone. Friends, Relations, Strangers, Friends of Strangers. If they can breathe, then they're a prospect.

The reality is, of course that, whilst such volumes of connections will produce a higher number of conversions, there will be a much larger volume of rejections that come with it.

It is, of course, important that you work through any fears you have about rejection. I used to have such a crippling fear of interrupting people and being disliked as a result, that I physically couldn't phone someone that wasn't expecting my call. It required some quite radical therapy work to get over it and now I can happily pick the phone up and chat to anyone.

Therefore, you do want to ensure that any underlying emotional barriers are removed but, even so, that doesn't mean you'll enjoy getting rejected.

Unless you are that special kind of breed, the reality is that the more "No's" you get, the more demoralised you're going to become. The more the resistance there will be around growing your business.

Also, as mentioned earlier, it's a pretty old fashioned and inefficient way of doing things.

Today, standard marketing processes focus on picking out a specific target market. As ever, it can swing too far the other way and you find some people who obsess about drilling down into the most specific of niches. Nevertheless, getting clear about who you want to work with just makes so much sense.

The best thing to do is focus on people that you know you would relate to anyway.

If you're a mother, focus on mothers. If you're into sport, focus on sporty people.

One of my clients focussed on joggers and dog walkers. Why? Because she walked her dog every day and jogged in the afternoon and would be continually entering into conversations with other people in the park.

By only thinking about a specific category of people, she really got to understand – via research as well as by talking to them – what their issues were and the key phrases to use that would stop people in their tracks and enter into conversation.

Eventually, she had no qualms about going into a park she'd never visited before and just going straight up to joggers and dog walkers that were total strangers. Within seconds she'd be in a deep engaging conversation.

Another example was a mum with a young child whose husband did shift work. They didn't earn enough to afford childcare, so the child went everywhere with her.

Who was she really good at speaking to? Mothers with kids trailing around after them. If their husbands also happened to be shift workers, then double bubble. She understood people in that position, talked about it, related to them, empathised, built trust, demonstrated how she'd made her business work for her and got them interested.

When you target the right type of person, you discover you just enjoy talking to them. Now you're not marketing or selling, you're connecting.

In fact, you don't even need to sell half the time. If they're interested, they will ask you about it.

Of course, you still get "No's", but the process is so much more enjoyable and, of course, the results are a lot better.

Find your target market and enjoy connecting with them.

CHAPTER 19
ONLY WORK WITH PEOPLE YOU WANT TO WORK WITH

In the previous chapter, we looked at the hazards of approaching anyone and everyone and getting a load of 'No's.

The other downside of the scattergun approach is that you also get a load of 'Yes's.

"What's wrong with that?" I hear you cry. Well, if your criteria for entry is 'breathing and the ability to say Yes', then you will end up with a big team of which about 20% will be performing.

The rules of nature mean that, of course, you will be spending all your energies managing the other lot.

It is important that you don't accept just anyone.

Instead, you want to filter your prospects for their attitude and abilities, as if you were recruiting for an important and high paid job.

For example, imagine you have two seemingly identical people in terms of circumstance. A single mum on the breadline, perhaps. There is nothing in or around their situation that will tell you which one will become the superstar and which one is on a pattern of self destruction.

You want to be able to give more of your time to the

one that's going to be successful – and work it out quickly. You don't want to be treating them exactly the same at the start, rushing in giving all of your time to both equally.

It may not be possible to judge these books by their cover but it is better if you can quickly suss them out, or else you're going to waste a lot of time.

Try putting 'hurdles' in the way when they want to sign up, to make sure they're really keen.

In my coaching business, I sometimes use a contract that includes a Test on my key terms and conditions. They have to pass this test before I'll work with them. On the one hand it makes sure that they've understood the key elements I want them to note, on the other, anyone who balks at taking a simple test, isn't going to be a good client for me.

It's only a little hurdle, but it can filter out a few unwanted people at an early stage.

What are the values you seek in a good team member and what sort of actions would a person with those values take?

What indicators can you look out for that will suggest that they will be the right kind of person?

Did they actually look at the video you sent them when they said they were going to? Did they respond to your email promptly and with enthusiasm? Did they show up at your monthly introductory meeting early and take notes and ask questions throughout?

When it looks like they are truly interested, then start to invest some proper time, but always be on the look out for danger signals.

When they ask for help, have they put the effort in and already tried from other sources? Did they watch the videos that were already available to them? Or are they just coming to you as an easy answer?

You may need to experience some bad ones in order to learn from them and know what those signals are, so don't despair for any that slip through. They provide an opportunity to learn.

But your time is important and they need to earn that time. Remember about setting the dogs on anyone that isn't going to help you build your future?

What hurdles can you put in place?

It might be simple things – make them come to you instead of the other way round. That tests their desire a lot more.

Say that you limit the number of people that you bring on each year and make them formally apply.

You can be as creative and as obstructive as you want, so have some fun with it.

Your best team members will not only buy into the product, but they'll also buy into you. Which means that other distributors are not a competition. Anyone who falls at one of your hurdles and joins another team is clearly someone you didn't want on your team.

Will this restrict the number of people who join?

Yes. That is the whole idea. Again, we're talking about quality over quantity.

The reality is that big non-performing teams are demoralising.

The counterintuitive bit is that, the harder you make it to join your team, the more exclusive it appears and the more the right people will want to join it.

Once they've made their way over all of your hurdles, you can be pretty sure that they're going to be motivated to make it work.

As they say, there is no queue for the wise man sat at the bottom of the mountain.

When you restrict entry to only those you want to work with, everyone just enjoys what they're doing so much more and, with enjoyment, comes better results.

CHAPTER 20
DON'T BE TOO PASSIONATE

This chapter may have some geographical variations. I'm talking from a UK perspective and appreciate that, in other countries (I'm looking at you, USA), this may be less of an issue, but pick out anything that may be relevant to you.

Quite frankly, in the UK, we don't do passion.

Anyone having a "freaking awesome day" is going to be looked at with huge amounts of suspicion and quietly ostracised from the community.

"What are they on?"

If you call me up and tell me that you've got something "really exciting" to show me, my cynic chip is going to kick in and the defences will be well and truly raised.

"Sorry mate, I'll be the judge as to whether it's exciting or not."

When you turn up to the network meeting in the branded car, wearing the branded polo shirt, drinking out of the branded mug – or even better, the branded drinking bottle, just £9.99 to you today – then quite frankly you come across as a religious zealot or the leader of a cult.

"Note to self - smile politely and avoid."

Then you get the network marketer who gets personally offended that I'm not interested in the product. To the extent that they get genuinely angry at the thought I may not part with some of my hard earned cash.

"My mistake. Now that you've physically threatened me, of course I'll enter into a business relationship with you."

In short, if you're over passionate when you speak to people, then you can very well put them off. Which can be difficult if you are truly and genuinely passionate about the product (which I kind of hope you are).

It's all a question of balance.

First of all, do a bit of research on matching and mirroring. There's plenty of free information about it on the internet. Ultimately, you are reacting to the person in front of you and adjusting your energy levels to be more closely matched with theirs. The aim is to find a level just above them, but not too much.

If they are a mild and quiet speaker, then slow down a bit and lower your voice slightly.

Then you can convert that passion of yours into an inner calm confidence. Be proud of the results, take joy in the success of others, but don't be impacted by the opinion of the person in front of you.

When you talk from that place of confidence and match the energy levels of the person you're speaking to, they will have the opportunity to discover the passion for themselves by experiencing results that changes their lives. The passion will never come from just being told about the product or the opportunity.

If they get it, then you can share in each other's excitement.

Otherwise, be mindful of the person in front of you, work out what is important to them and remember that too much passion closes ears.

CHAPTER 21
YOU'RE SELLING OYSTERS

Just to let you know, I don't like oysters. Never had one, never going to. You'll never sell me oysters, so don't try to.

On the other hand, I do like sausage rolls. Ooh! I love a sausage roll. Got any sausage rolls for sale?

All right, last time I checked there wasn't a network marketing organisation specialising in food. Maybe one does exist, but clearly that's not my point.

The thing is, there are some things that I have no interest in. Regardless of whether I've tried them or not, I'm going to have a pretty good idea whether or not it's the sort of thing I'm going to like.

If you try to sell me oysters, I'll say no.

And it's ok for me to say no.

It's not a big deal. It's not a reflection on the quality of the oyster. I don't have an issue with you. I just don't want any oysters.

In which case, you should move on and find someone who might like oysters.

And that is what is going on with your products.

There are just some people who won't want them,

no matter what you say or do.

And that is ok.

I remember interviewing someone when doing some extra research for this book and she was a distributor of a well known healthcare organisation.

Being who she was, once the interview was over she wanted to pique my interest in her products.

Now, I'm a pretty old fashioned traditional bloke when it comes to my 'grooming regime'. In other words, I don't have one.

"No fuss, no bother" is my motto. Own brand shampoo and shower gel for 99p from the local supermarket – as long as people can cope with standing within a foot or two of me, I'm doing a good job.

Now, I told her this, but she was dead set on trying to get me to try her wonderful, expensive shampoo. Pushing me with arguments about "what you put in your hair ends up in your body."

Then I was being sold on how to maintain my youthful looks and the ideal face cream for me. How the pores would replenish and plumpen and leave me glowing and refreshed.

Or some such stuff.

I didn't actually have any issue with the things she

was saying. It all sounded sensible and correct.

Just not something that interests me.

"But it SHOULD interest you" cry those in the industry.

Maybe. But it doesn't. Deal with it and move on.

Of course, the more this lady tried to get me to try things, the more I started to resist and, by the end of it, a friendly and positive conversation ended up leaving a bit of a bad taste in my mouth ("Hey, try our minty fresh toothpaste").

A softer approach was unlikely to yield any different result, but at least I'd have felt better disposed towards her and, who knows, if things changed in the future, I may well have gone back to her. Remote chance, possibly, but a chance none the less.

As opposed to the zero chance situation we now find ourselves in.

Remember. You're selling oysters. Some people don't like oysters. If someone says they don't like oysters, don't force feed them oysters !!

You'll enjoy what you do so much more when you sell to people who want it.

PART 5

How To Stay Positive And Enjoy Life

CHAPTER 22
CELEBRATE THE LITTLE SUCCESSES

There's nothing new around the concept of 'celebrating your successes'. It's a common trope, but there can be a tendency to only focus on the big wins and forget the little things that are going on underneath.

Like the Great Barrier Reef: lots of tiny, almost invisible, things come together and add up to something massive.

The company machine is programmed to reward people and success, but the high profile celebrations are targeted at big results. The top earners; the biggest team growth; the most new clients. These are the ones that get applauded on stage.

From this place, it can be very easy to slip into a state of shame and embarrassment around the fact that you've ONLY got 4 team members. Or that my team members ONLY buy stuff for themselves.

However, these are the little things that underpin everything. Don't apologise for it – celebrate it.

Every comparison that you ever make should only be against where you started – zero. Everything else is irrelevant. Any achievement above this base point is worthy of celebration and recognition.

What is more, instead of celebrating the results, celebrate the actions. When you put 5 calls in or hold 5 conversations, give yourself a pat on the back, regardless of the outcome.

No-one has control over what people will do or say, so celebrating results is like saying "well done for being lucky." Be grateful for the luck when it comes, but congratulate yourself for things that you have total control over i.e. what you do and say.

When you start to focus on small positive behavioural points, then it leads to the proliferation of good behaviour, which encourages you to do more and so the business grows.

In addition to motivating yourself, you should bear in mind the progress of your team members. Make sure that you help them celebrate the small actions that they take.

Make sure you reward them, even if the system doesn't.

CHAPTER 23
CELEBRATE YOUR FAILURES

Sounds like a contradiction from the previous chapter?

In many ways, it's exactly the same thing, because you should be looking to celebrate the actions you take not the outcome, so any action is worthy of celebration, which includes the failures.

However, there is an extra dimension at work here and that is to literally be glad when things go wrong. Particularly if you're a perfectionist.

First of all, we kind of know that we have to fail in order to learn. Every time we fell down when learning to walk or stalled the car when learning to drive, was essential to install the correct procedures that we now take for granted. Every success comes through trying new things and persevering.

If you were at the peak of your abilities, then you would be getting everything right every time and you would be perfect. That would mean you would have nowhere to go. No room for improvement. Consequently, the life you're leading is as good as it gets and you're stuck with the results that you're currently getting.

This means that when we make mistakes and fail, we have just discovered an opportunity to improve.

It gives hope that there are more things to learn and shows you the areas where you can get even better, which can only lead to better results.

If you want to be the best you can be, then you need to be actively seeking out the failures. It will mean that you are pushing yourself and, as long as you learn from those mistakes, you are going to be continually on an upward curve.

It should be balanced with the successes, naturally, but use failures at the edge of your comfort zone as a compass that can guide you to better things.

Now that is worth celebrating.

CHAPTER 24
DON'T EXPECT TO BE BELIEVED

You are given training and scripts that will walk your prospect through a dream life that they've always wanted. It will give them everything they could ever imagine – happiness, prosperity and freedom.

You back it up with evidence and statistics, testimonials from independent third parties and, of course, your own honest and most heartfelt story as to how and why this business, this product, has saved your life.

They have nodded at the correct bits, said yes at the right times and then, once the 'no-brainer' presentation has been completed, you ask them if they'd like to join and they say

"Erm ... No thank you."

Obviously, they rarely actually say "No." It's more likely to be "Can I think about it...I'll get back to you" and so on, but you get my point.

How stupid do some people have to be to ignore a perfect opportunity sat right in front of their face?

The reality is, of course, is that we are conditioned to focus on the negatives. We assume that everyone is out for themselves and that they pose a threat to us. This was a basic evolutionary tactic.

Those people who trusted anyone and everyone they met, didn't get to pass their genes on to the next generation.

In short, we are conditioned to disbelieve anything positive.

The whole "If it's too good to be true, it probably is" philosophy.

Here's a thought experiment that is worth considering. As a note, if anyone reading this decides to actually carry out the experiment, I'd love to hear the results.However, I imagine people have done enough talking to people in the street to accept the results as laid out here.

The experiment runs like this.

Go and stand in a reasonably busy high street with a bundle of £10 notes. Pull one out and hold it up, nice and clear for everyone to see.

As people wander by, try and stop them with words along the lines of:

"Excuse me, I'm conducting an experiment and am giving away £10 notes to anyone that talks to me."

Now, see how long it takes to get rid of all the £10 notes.

You will give away all of the money eventually, but it will take a lot longer than one might imagine.

Certainly more than just asking 10 people. Most people will shuffle away, ignore you, keep their heads down and pick up the pace or whatever method they use to avoid talking to strangers accosting them in the street.

There can be no argument about the value of what you're offering. There are no catches, no tricks, no consequences, but people will still not believe you.

Eventually, someone will engage. They will be very hesitant, they'll ask questions and finally, after much consideration, they will take the £10.

If others are watching, things might now move quite quickly. Once one person has seen that it's safe, they'll all flood in. Or even ask for more than one, once the confidence kicks in.

Consequently, anything other than a thought experiment makes this quite an expensive way to prove a point.

But it is important to remember that when you're trying to sell something to someone, it has nothing to do with who you are, nothing to do with how good the product is, nothing to do with how you present – there are some people who just won't believe you.

Accept that fact now and it will avoid you a whole boat load of stress.

CHAPTER 25
YOU ARE A GOD/GODDESS

Now, before you shut the book and throw it in the bin thinking you've been tricked into reading the ramblings of a mad man, let me explain.

Traditionally, there are two types of god (with a small 'g').

There is god as 'creator'. The type that can pull pieces together, either from what is around or out of the aether, and manifest thoughts, things, concepts, peoples and worlds. Making something out of nothing.

Then there is the god as 'influencer'. The type that gets involved on a day to day basis - not always obvious, but can manipulate things to suit whatever divine purpose he or she holds.

Ok. Here is the kicker.

You are a god. Or a goddess. As am I, and so is everyone on the planet, for that matter. Let me explain.

In the first instant, I believe that we all create our own world.

Our brains are designed to filter and interpret what goes on around us in a way that we can make sense of. The reality of life is very different to what we perceive.

When you hold this book, you think you're touching it. In reality, none of your cells are touching the cells of the book (or e-reader), it's actually very strong electromagnetic forces keeping the cells of your hand at a distance from the cells of the book. Our brain simply interprets it in a way that makes sense i.e. touch.

When you look out of the window, you think that you're seeing the world as it is. In fact, you're only seeing a select few things, because if you saw every bit of information that is coming through your eyes, you'd be overwhelmed. The brain filters and sorts it for you. Even then, all that's coming through is light reflecting off of other objects in various ways and, as certain dresses have proved on social media, not everyone sees things in the same way.

Most importantly is how we create what we feel. When we hear somebody make a comment, see somebody do something, or imagine the consequences of an action, every single thought and emotion that we have around those situations is completely fabricated internally. It will be based on previous experiences, assumptions and half truths – rarely on reality.

Consequently, pretty much everything we touch, everything we see and everything we experience in the world has been created inside our own minds.

Secondly, we clearly have an influence on our daily lives. Often in ways that we don't even realise.

The majority of our actions and decisions are

actually carried out via subconscious patterns and automatic routines. We take it for granted that we do many things automatically, such as breathing, but actions such as making a definitive decision, is not as clear cut as it seems.

Studies have shown that our subconscious drives the majority of our decision making and that our logical, conscious brains simply justify the decision that's already been made.

Tests have been done where subjects are placed in an MRI scanner and given a decision to make. For example, "do you want tea or coffee?"

Via the scanner it is possible to see at which point the brain settles down on the route it's going to take and has made a decision. Meanwhile, the subject has to press a button when they are sure they've made a decision.

There is a significant gap between the two results. In some cases as much as 10 seconds.

Every single time, the decision ended up being the one that the brain settled on first.

When we get caught in life's traps, repeating the same mistakes over and over again, it is because we are running automatic programmes without any conscious awareness of what we are doing.

Luckily, we can change the programming because, as we know, we create our own world. I'm not saying it's easy, but it can be done.

Trying new things, driving new habits, deliberately taking steps you wouldn't normally take. All of these are launchpads for creating new neural pathways, new programming and a new world.

Returning to the theme of this chapter, all of this means that you create your own world and influence everything that you do, think or feel.

Which means that you are a god.

There is, of course, a caveat. And that is, that you are only god of your own world. You can't create or control anyone else. You only have domain over yourself.

But, to be honest, five minutes ago you didn't even know you were a god, so I think being god of anything is pretty cool. Right?

So. Here we are. You are god of your own world.

You can be, do or have anything you could possibly imagine. You can create miracles with the click of your fingers.

So, Almighty one. Over to you.

What do you want? What miracles would you like to perform?

CHAPTER 26
LESS SELF-ISH AND MORE SELF

One of the common challenges that runs through a number of areas in this book is that in order to have a successful and enjoyable life, we have to put our own needs ahead of others.

This can be a challenge for many of us.

Looking to follow a life of wealth and happiness by recommending products to our friends that will directly benefit ourselves, can be incredibly uncomfortable for some people. Our parents, teachers and the books we read as children went to great lengths to tell us not to be selfish and to think of others before ourselves. If this obsession around selfishness becomes fully internalised, the results can be crippling.

How dare we actually get what we want?

Many of the techniques to overcome this revolve around the idea of considering the win-win nature of any commercial relationship, in an attempt to remove some of the guilt. A common analogy is that of the flight safety announcement on an aeroplane and that, in the event of the oxygen masks coming down from the ceiling, your job is to put YOUR OWN mask on first and THEN help other people.

If we do not look after ourselves, then we can not look after others. On the assumption that what you do is genuinely beneficial, then it is your duty to look after number one in the first instance, in order to help more people.

This shift in perception can be quite useful as it changes the balance between parties and you can justify your actions internally.

However, it doesn't deal with the underlying issues around selfishness itself, so let's see if we can help with that.

Let's imagine two young children: a brother and sister for argument's sake; sat on the living room floor, whilst the mother is keeping one eye on them and trying to get some work done at the same time.

The brother has a bag of sweets and his younger sister is badgering him to let her have one. As you would expect, it ends up in a fight with much wailing and gnashing of (baby) teeth.

Mum wades in, checks out the situation and tells her son to just give his sister a sweet.

"Don't be selfish", she might say. "Share with your sister".

Now, how you view this will depend on your personal experience.

It could be argued that the brother is being selfish for not sharing his sweets.

Someone else might say that the sister is being

selfish, for trying to get something that isn't hers.

Meanwhile, it's not ridiculous to say that the mother is being selfish, because she wants the kids to shut up, so that she can get on with what she's doing.

However you look at it, you can find a culprit. Everyone is, arguably, being selfish.

In fact, in any situation, there is never just one person being selfish.

I can **only** be selfish if I end up with something at **your** expense. By definition, the alternative situation is that **you** end up with something at **my** expense, which thereby makes **you** selfish.

The truth is that selfishness is just a perspective, a point of view – not an absolute.

I do not accept, therefore, that in any given situation you can say that you are being selfish.

You could say, however, that you are choosing to look at the situation in such a way that makes it **appear** as if you're being selfish.

That is quite a different statement and allows you to make a decision. From the last chapter, we know that you can make a choice as to how you look at things and react to them. You have control over your inner perceptions.

Is there a way that you can look at your situation

such that someone else is being selfish?

You may think that you are being selfish in wanting to sell your products to make some money. Surely though, doesn't your customer crave a better figure or a more beautiful appearance (depending on what your product is). Are they not being selfish for wanting what you're selling?

In any given situation, you can shift your perspective and realise that you are not putting your needs ahead of others.

Now incorporate the importance of looking after yourself in order to help others and you may be able to worry less about being self-ish and concentrate on the self.

CHAPTER 27
SOME ANSWERS ARE NOT FOUND IN BOOKS

There is a trap that everyone falls into at some point or another, particular when you are keen and eager to develop and improve.

The desire to learn about growth can actually get in the way of growth.

Seminars, books, training, coaching, audios, videos – there is so much information out there that trying to take it all in can become a full time job in itself.

Suddenly, you find that you're spending so much time learning, that you're not actually **doing** anything.

The truth of the matter is that you haven't really learnt something just because you can recite back a key phrase or explain a concept. True learning comes from testing it out in the real world. Taking the ideas that have come your way and shoving and adapting them so that they work for you. Or, of course, been sufficiently tested to know that it isn't right for you.

Very often, this educational trap comes about because the person in question is using learning as an excuse. It is a great way to appear busy without having to face the reality of having to go out there and actually face the world, which is usually the genuine fear going on beneath.

If there is some sort of underlying fear that prevents you from taking action, then nothing you learn will work, as you're not really learning it. This can result in you hopping from one seminar to the next, on a self delusional pursuit for the holy grail – the answer that will solve all your problems – something that gets you the results without you having to take the action.

This, of course, does not exist.

True learning does not lie in a book or a video course. It lies within.

Take some time out to look at yourself and what you've been learning. Have you actually been applying the things that you've been taught before moving on?

If not, then you might want to re-evaluate your strategy.

Be more selective in choosing what to read, watch or attend. Not everything is right for you.

Don't go to an event just because everyone else is, or it's been heavily recommended by your upline. Only pay for programmes and events (books, training, coaching) where you genuinely expect to use the teaching. Building in, of course, time afterwards to apply anything that may come out of them.

Select for quality not quantity. Remember, just

because the company puts it on, doesn't mean that it's going to be the thing you need. Much more might be achieved from an external course that may give you a different perspective. Whilst this increases the number of things to look at, it highlights even more the importance of being selective.

When you hear someone talk about 'something that worked for them' don't automatically assume that it will work for you. Try and limit the nuggets you take forwards.

Change your mantra from "learn, learn, learn" to "Learn – do, Learn – do, Learn – do".

I will finish this chapter with a quote from Jim Kwik that I'm rather fond of:

"If an egg is broken from an outside force, life ends.

If an egg is broken from an inside force, life begins.

Great things always begin from inside. "

CHAPTER 28
YOU ARE ALLOWED TO CHANGE
"YOUR WAY"

The purpose of this book is to help you break away from the mindset that you have to do things the way that others have done them, so that you can take control of your own life and find your own "Way" of doing things.

An essential part of this is that, once you have found a way that works for you, not to become trapped by it.

We often feel that, when we've strived for something and achieved it, then we need to stick to our guns and defend that position. That to deviate from that line will be a breach of our values and allow others to wail "But you said ..."

One of the major root causes of business failure, in any industry, is to try and grow without making appropriate changes. The growth of a business is limited to the amount of changes that the owner makes, so the owner needs to grow personally in order for the business to follow suit.

There is a good book by Marshall Goldsmith called "What Got You Here, Won't Get You There" which outlines the number of times that businesses struggle because they keep following successful patterns from the past, instead of developing new thinking, which is required if they want to go further.

By the way, if you have taken on board the contents of Chapter 27, don't go out and buy that book just because I mentioned it.

The point is that you are in control and, if at some future point you want to change things, then that is fine.

Even if that decision is to quit !

We change as people, so our "Way" can change too. What doesn't work for us today, may work for us tomorrow - and vice versa.

So always keep exploring and don't be afraid of adjusting, adding and subtracting from what you do.

Happy hunting and may you find "Your Way".

PART 6

Do Something Different To Get A Different Result

JOIN ANDREW MILLER AT A "BREATHING SPACE"

Get involved with a FREE online discussion group dedicated to helping each other enjoy business.

Book on at www.bit.ly/CommunityWEB

How do some people run a successful business AND maintain a genuine sense of contentment? How do they enjoy what they do?

For many of us, our fantasy image of the happy, successful entrepreneur, hasn't really played out as we hoped, but we don't know how to put things right.

Enjoying every aspect of our work and life is a reality that's within reach of all of us, if we're prepared to stretch our muscles and try something new!

The Breathing Spaces are inclusive groups where we take time out from our busy schedules once a month to explore how to combine happiness, purpose and enjoyment into our work and personal lives.

We all crave enjoyment in life. To find it, there are four key needs that must be met:
- Safety;
- Belonging;
- Esteem; and
- Purpose.

Understanding how we can meet those needs means we're well on the way to fulfilling them.

We focus on a different theme each month:
- Enjoying Business   - Finding Your Purpose
- Finding Your Tribe   - Feeling Safe
- Inner Confidence   - Money Hangups

At each meeting, we help each other to remove the blocks to enjoyment and help to create a connection between our actions and what we want to achieve in life.

The Breathing Spaces were initially formed as physical groups and it is always worth checking the website to see if there is one near you.

However, no matter where you are based, you will be able to access the **FREE** webinars that I run once a month and I would love to welcome you to join us on the next one.

PLUS THERE IS A "NO UPSELL" GUARANTEE:
This is **NOT** one of those webinars designed to lure you in and then plug some sort of programme at the end. It is about building a community of people who believe that there is more to life than just money.

As for myself, my mission is to change the conversation such that success in business is measured by how much you enjoy it, not just how much money you make.

Once you get everything in place, the feeling is like nothing you've ever felt before. It's like a lightning bolt shooting through the key elements of your body - your Brain, your Tummy and your Soul - collectively known by their initials as "Your Bits".

For more information and links to the booking page, simply go to:

www.businessenjoyment.com/breathingspaces

If you want to know what really makes you happy; if you want things in your life to change; join us and learn how to enjoy your life and the success you've worked hard for.

I want you to enjoy your business so much it makes 'Your Bits' tingle.

Testimonial for the Breathing Spaces

My main concern about attending a Breathing Space was maybe it was going to be high pressured or salesy, with people trying to sell you a product or get you to buy into their business.

But it's not been like that at all.

I found it really welcoming. Quite a diverse group of people with lots of different skill sets.

The way the session was structured was really informative though quite informal, relaxed and, of course, enjoyable.

I think the information given throughout the session was really useful and I like the fact that the group gave some really useful pointers as well. It was very supportive and you were able to think, take it in and reflect, which I thought was very effective.

From today I've got a clear plan of action of what I need to do. For me, it's solidified what my passion and vision is and confirmed that what I am doing is the right thing. I just need to give it my all.

Honestly, I feel inspired.

Karen Fallis
Nutritionist

Other comments about Breathing Space

"Valuable time to take a step back and reflect on lots of things with an excellent group, giving us an opportunity to learn from other people's experiences and help others if we can."

"This is the only place I go online and I don't stick makeup on my face"

"Utterly fabulous!"

"Deep. Very reflective. Thought provoking."

"A useful timeout to reflect and notice how I'm feeling, about and within myself. And space to decide what I want to change or do more of."

"A breath of fresh air during a busy work and home life. They make one stop and think differently about my direction and happiness."

"Phenomenal"

"Truly Life Changing"

APPENDIX
DOMESTIC DISPUTES

This is not really a section that one would expect to find in a book about Network Marketing. In Chapter 2, I touched on the possibility of something deeper going on within a relationship and it wasn't right to cover it there for that very reason. That's not what this book is about.

However, having opened up that particular can and because I've seen it happen in the real world, I felt it only responsible to at least acknowledge what I'd hinted at and to provide some sort of solution for those who need it.

Before I continue, I should make it clear that I am not a marriage guidance counsellor or trained for dealing with abusive relationships, so my conclusions will all be around talking to someone professional. However, if I can help you to identify what is going on (which isn't always apparent) it might help you to have the right conversation with the right person.

There are four key questions that you should consider. Be honest with yourself – you don't need to reveal your answers to anyone at this stage.

Are you safe physically?

The most important question that we need to ask up front and it's not as easy an answer as one might think.

If you ever feel scared of being physically hurt or things are happening which result in you being bruised or in pain, then you need to speak to someone immediately. Your doctor would be a good starting point. In extreme cases, there are helplines and, of course, the police.

This may seem obvious advice to those who aren't experiencing it, but the truth of the matter is that people in an abusive relationship frequently refuse to accept the seriousness of the situation and will find excuses for their partner's behaviour. Usually through fear of the alternative. For example, the fear of being alone is so massive that being with anyone is better than being with no-one.

It is not acceptable for any form of violence to be used, in any situation, so if this is you, ignore all of the voices that say otherwise and speak to someone now.

Are you safe psychologically?

This is a lot more subtle to identify though it can, in many ways, be just as damaging.

Does your other half try to control you or insult you verbally?

Maybe they control the bank account and won't give you access to money that is rightfully yours. Perhaps they take every opportunity to drag you down – calling you stupid, ugly or worthless.

Do they prevent you from going out and meeting your friends or having a social life apart from them?

All of these can be forms of psychological abuse and are all fear based tactics designed to control you. However, things can be a lot more subtle and less clear in this arena and it is important to be able to distinguish between very mild controlling tactics and just peculiar habits. For example, you may have one person in a relationship who is responsible for all of the bank accounts and they may be a bit obsessive about it, but that may not run into the arena of being actual abuse.

If you suspect anything along these lines, once gain, talk to your doctor. They can refer you to a professional who can help you ascertain what is a genuine threat to you and what is just someone being a little overzealous.

Are you both ok?

If there are no actual threats to you then we can move onto issues that are more balanced and deal with the relationship itself.

If you are in a relationship where you are continually arguing, then one of two things is going on. Either you're not suited for each other or one of you is having a very difficult time and is just lashing out.

First of all then, are you ok?

Take some time out and really sit down to think

about how you feel. There will be the natural fears and anxieties of life, especially if you're starting out on new ventures and pushing yourself outside of your comfort zone. However, deep down, beneath it all ... how are you actually?

Then think about your other half. Are they ok? What's going on in their life? Can you see any reason for them to be stressed? When was the last time they opened up to you and gave you an insight into what they were really feeling?

In either case, if you think there may be need for professional support, raise it with your doctor and see what they suggest.

If you're sure that both of you are, essentially, ok, then maybe it's just a cycle of bad habits. Think about how the arguments start.

How they really start.

Every argument arises from a misunderstanding or a miscommunication, frequently due to an assumption being made by one or both of the parties. The truth is often very different.

One definition of an argument is two people, both of whom are wrong, but think that they're more right than the other person.

Maybe it's the look that they give or the tone of voice they use that you interpret in a certain way. Maybe it's the look that YOU give or the tone of voice that YOU use, that they interpret in their way.

See if you can experiment with deliberately not rising to their anger and see what happens. Or, as difficult and as frustrating as it may be, have a go at admitting you are wrong and they are right – even if you know that it isn't the case.

Not easy, I know, but if you're arguing over stupid things, then recognise that and accept it doesn't matter. By playing a different role, you are breaking the established patterns which may end up in a different outcome.

You may find that they calm down and you can then have a mature, 'establish the facts' style conversation.

If you know that you essentially have a good relationship and truly want it to continue, then an open dialogue between the two of you really is the solution to everything. If they aren't in the habit of such conversations, they won't suddenly change overnight and start opening up. It may take some coaxing.

However, one of you has to start behaving differently by being more open and you're the one reading this book, so it probably ought to start with you.

Do you really want to be with them?

We usually don't ask ourselves the difficult

questions because we're scared what the answer might be. It is, however, a truth that sometimes people drift apart or the relationship was never right in the first place.

There are plenty of excuses for people to stay together even when they aren't right for each other:

- I made a vow and I meant it;
- What would my parents think?;
- anything else would mean that I'd failed;
- my other half would be upset if we broke up;

and so on.

Given all of that, take a moment to really think hard. Irrespective of what other people would think or how it may be wrong - do you truly, genuinely still want to be in a relationship with this person? Why did you fall in love with them in the first place? What do you admire about them? Why are you really still together?

If the answer is yes, you do want to be with them, then great. You've got something to focus on and you can consider exploring marriage guidance counselling or the points raised in the previous section.

If the answer, in reality, is no. Then you've got some serious decisions to make. There will be therapists, coaches, counsellors out there that can help you think about it but, at the end of the day, it's going to be a decision that you have to make and you'll have to be at peace with the possible consequences.

Summary

As stated at the start, I'm not an expert in this area and the solutions usually involve talking to someone else – be that your doctor, a counsellor or your other half themselves.

Very rarely are there easy answers, otherwise you wouldn't have the issue in the first place, which means that none of your choices appear attractive. The alternative is, of course, to do absolutely nothing and leave things exactly the way they are. However, that is still a decision and you won't be doing yourself any favours.

As per Chapter 26, there are times when you have to put yourself first and work out what the right thing for you is. Beneath everything, if you want things to change, you're going to have to speak to somebody about it.

You just need to decide on who.

www.ingramcontent.com/pod-product-compliance
Lightning Source LLC
Chambersburg PA
CBHW060849170526
45158CB00001B/285